SELLING AND MANAGING FOR A LUXURY EXPERIENCE

Sales Training for Professionals

BRUCE EICHER

Copyright © 2009 Bruce Eicher
All rights reserved.

ISBN: 1-4392-3283-0
EAN13: 9781439232835

Visit www.booksurge.com to order additional copies.

DEDICATION

To Katie, Nick, and Tay, whose love, support, and assistance made all this possible.

TABLE OF CONTENTS

INTRODUCTION III
HOW TO USE THIS BOOK 1
    MANAGE YOURSELF 1
    A TRAINING SCHEDULE 2
USE YOUR SELLING SYSTEM 5
    ADD THE LAYER OF LUXURY 5
    SAMPLE SELLING SYSTEM + L.E. LESSONS 6
CHOOSE YOUR POSITION 7
    SELF FULFILLED PROPHECY 7
    POSITIVE RESPONSE 7
    IT'S THAT SIMPLE 8
CREATE AN OASIS 11
    MY OASIS 11
    TRANSPLANT THE OASIS AT WORK 13
    WELCOMING IMPRESSIONS 13
    OPEN SPACES, ALLURING PATHS 14
    CREATE A TRANQUIL ATMOSPHERE 15
    WOW THEM UNEXPECTEDLY 16
    MEMORIES TO SHARE 17
MAKE AND SEIZE OPPORTUNITY 21
    THE CLERK 21
    THE SALES PROFESSIONAL 22
    WHAT WENT RIGHT 23
    FLATTER AND EXCITE ALL GUESTS 24
    NEVER STOP SELLING 26
SERVE AND THEY WILL COME 31
    OUR COMPETITION 31
    PROMOTE FROM WITHIN 31
    THE LUXURY EXPERIENCE SERVICE CALL 32

THE LUXURY EXPERIENCE CLIENT BOOK. 37
PERSONAL SERVICE RECORD. 38
Guest Information. 40
Items of Interest 41
Other Notes 41
A Bird in the Hand. 41
Purchase History and Follow-Up 42
Guest Services 43
Alpha Tabs and Follow-Up Pending 44
Planning Calendar and Delivery Log 45
Life Events 45
Sales Goals and More 46
MONTHLY EVENTS 49
SPECIAL ORDER/SERVICE DELIVERY LOG 50
SALES PLANNER, YEAR. 51
SALES PLANNER, MONTH. 52

A LUXURY E-MAIL EXPERIENCE 55
Etiquette Rules. 55
Sample E-Mail 62

HARNESS THE POWER OF EMOTIONS 63
Why People Shop and Buy 63
Life Moments. 63
The Two Types of Needs 64
Clerked Transaction. 64
I'm Just Looking 65
Fill the Emotional Need. 66
The Gifting Moment. 67
Awaken the Analytical 68

BUILDING VALUE ABOVE THE PRICE 73
The Anxiety of Price. 73
Our Confidence Is Paramount 73
Price Is a Functional Need 74
Value Is an Emotional Need 75
Past the Register. 76
Selling Luxury Goods. 77
We All Need a Story 78

CLOSE ON THE EMOTIONAL HIGH 83
WATCH THE SIGNS 83
USE AN ASSUMPTION CLOSE 84
KEEP THEM IN THE LIFE MOMENT 85
NOTHING TO LOOSE 85

MORE CLIENTS, MORE OFTEN, SPENDING MORE MONEY 89
80% FROM 20% 89
KNOW YOUR TOP 20 PERCENT 90
KNOW WHEN, WHERE, AND WHY YOUR TOP 20 PERCENT SPEND THEIR MONEY 91
KEEP THE 20 PERCENT HAPPY 91
CULTIVATE AND HARVEST UNCOVERED OPPORTUNITIES 92
GROOM TOMORROW'S 20 PERCENT 93
ASK FOR REFERRALS 93
DO NOT CATER TO THE EXCEPTIONS 94
ANOTHER STORY 94

SUCCESS WITH TEAMWORK 99
COMMI$$ION$ VS THE LUXURY EXPERIENCE 99
ALL HANDS ON DECK 100
TEAM SELLING 100
THE TURN OVER PROCESS 101
TURN OVER VS TEAM SELL 106
EVERYWHERE THERE ARE SIGNS 106
STEPS TO THE T.O. 108
SALES FLOOR ETIQUETTE 109

SELLING AGAINST THE INTERNET 113
WHAT'S NEW ABOUT THE INTERNET? 113
QUESTIONS ON THEIR MIND 114
PLANT THE SEED OF DOUBT 117
KNOWLEDGE IS POWER 118
IF YOU CAN'T BEAT THEM, JOIN THEM 118

CREATE YOUR CULTURE AND LIVE YOUR DREAM 121
VISION STATEMENT 121
MISSION STATEMENT 122
SERVICE STANDARDS 123
LIVE YOUR DREAM 124

ACKNOWLEDGMENT

When I was only 19 years old, I managed my first retail business. It was a camera and photofinishing store in Southern Oregon. I learned right away that you have to give personal attention to your customers and share in their life's moments, even at the sales counter.

I also learned that sharing experiences works both ways and benefits us all. At my store I had the pleasure of helping a client, a guest by the name of Richard Bach. He would bring film in to be processed, photos taken on his fabulous adventure and share them with me as he looked them over. Richard seems to know how to live a good life and pursue his dreams. You could tell that from his photos, and his writings confirm my first impressions.

I can still remember a striking photo of Richard next to an airplane of his. I had always dreamed of flying my own airplane and his sharing meant more to me than he could know. It took me many years to bring my dream onto reality, but I have now held my private pilots license for eight years. I know now that if you want to succeed at anything but the simplest tasks, you have to apply passion, dedication and persistence, and that nothing easy reaps great rewards. It all starts with a desire and a goal.

"You are never given a wish without also being given the power to make it come true. You may have to work for it, however."

—*Richard Bach*

"*Between stimulus and response there is a space. In that space is our power to choose our response. In our response lies our growth and our freedom.*"

— *Viktor E. Frankl*

INTRODUCTION

The retail climate is changing. No longer do we have rampage consumerism funded by free flowing credit lines driving consumers to our cash registers. Whether that describes your core client or not, I believe we are all affected. Most companies are seeing some slowdown in business traffic and sales. And our clients are cautious, expecting more than ever in return for their hard earned dollar.

Now it is even more important to hold onto our market share and secure our clientele. If we take a wait and see attitude we will be further behind when we wake up. And if we just work on cutting our overhead expenses we will loose market share and give away our clients.

But if we take simple, low cost steps to improve the experience for our clients, we will advance our place in the market, secure loyalty from our clients, and be a leader in our field. We will have the pole position for the New Retail Climate.

So what is our opportunity? <u>Throughout the sales industry there is the lack of a luxury experience for the client.</u> The lessons in this book will clearly show you how to provide this much needed experience for our clients. We will become consultant salespeople that can capitalize on the emotion of spending money. We will be able to create more business from past clients and casual encounters. With this luxury experience a professional salesperson will build value in his or hers product way beyond its sticker price. And we will receive more referral business to catapult us into continued success.

The slow economy should be viewed as an opportunity. No great achievement or advancement has been made when everything is running smoothly. Adversity creates the need for change or invention. Real achievement is made when we face our adversity or challenge head-on. While our competitors are simply waiting for things to get better, or while they are cutting back staff, training, marketing, and consumer perks, not only will we hold our place but will gain market share and come out ahead of the pack and be positioned to advance quicker and further.

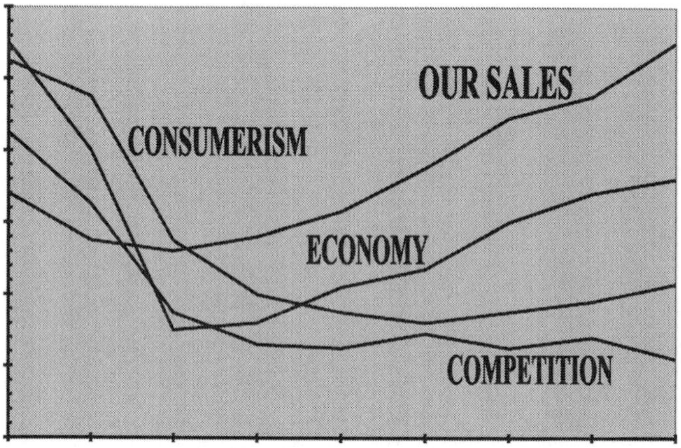
OUR SALES
CONSUMERISM
ECONOMY
COMPETITION

HOW TO USE THIS BOOK

The layout of the book is in chapters that will convert to weekly training meetings. As a manager, I always held my meetings on Saturday morning an hour or two before we opened our store. You can continue whatever schedule you have established. The important thing is to have a schedule and keep to it. Then after the meetings, practice the weekly lesson, implement the procedures, monitor the results, and follow up.

Manage Yourself

I wrote this book with the mindset that both sales associates and sales managers would be reading it. Reading is only the first step and if everyone has, then it can be reviewed with much more of a round-table discussion at the meetings. I have included paragraphs labeled; "Manager's Notes". I fully expect everyone to read these notes. Then you should all ask the question, "Is this an opportunity for change or action that I can use to better myself?" Then beat your supervisor to the punch and do it. <u>If one wants to excel and advance in his or her field of expertise, no matter their title, they must make themselves easy to manage.</u>

You will see I recommend a lot of practice in the form of role-plays. I can hear it now, "we all hate role-plays!" or, "role-plays aren't real life." You tell me, would you rather practice and stumble with your team-mates or with the one or two clients you will be lucky to see today? My wife and I role-play all the time; why not let your co-works have some of the fun too.

After you and your staff have read the book, cover to cover, we can get into a typical training week.

A Training Schedule

- Pick a chapter from the book and announce it as subject matter for your next sales meeting.
- Everyone; reread the chapter to be reviewed, noting ideas for discussion and techniques to be implemented.
- Delegate research and preparation for the meeting.
- Hold the meeting in a roundtable discussion format.

    - Read aloud to each other key points, and then open them up for discussion.
    - Discuss how these ideas would benefit everyone, and increase your business.
    - Ask for input on how to best apply these ideas and service standards in your business.
    - Get an agreement and commitment from everyone to make these changes.
    - Manager and volunteer(s) should lead off with a role-play for the group on these new procedures.
    - Continue role-plays as time allows.
    - Announce next chapter or lesson for next meeting.
    - Again review the commitment to change you have pledged and the benefits of these new service standards to your business.

- On the sales floor hold role-plays one-on-one and in team sessions so everyone has the opportunity to practice.
- Give feedback to each other; make changes as needed to smooth over the presentation to the client.
- Throughout the week monitor the sales floor, watch and listen to the interaction with your associates and clients.
- Give immediate feedback; praise in public, constructive criticize in private…

- Take note of all success stories, no matter how small. Catch them doing it right and praise them.
- At the next weeks meeting have everyone share their success stories using the new Service Standard. You will find this very powerful.
- Repeat this outline as needed to cover the book.

Selling is a lot of small things done to help a client make the decision to buy. Let's say there are 100 little things we should do to be successful. And each one of these things increases our chances by 1%. What would happen if we did them all?

USE <u>YOUR</u> SELLING SYSTEM

This book is not intended to rewrite yet another selling system. All salespeople, early in their careers learn a step by step selling system. I have worked with and taught many systems to my managers and associates. These systems can have five to fifteen steps and different names for the same steps. The point of a step by step system is to provide a ladder to success. Like climbing the ladder, missing a step at any given point you could fall. But if you place a foot up each step you will succeed.

I want you to use the selling system you have in place. You have invested time and money for your system and have at least some comfort and success using it. With my knowledge teaching salespeople we can provide another layer on the foundation of your selling steps. Think of it like upgrading your ladder to success for an escalator to triumph.

Add the Layer of Luxury

What I have found in these systems is a lack of a luxury experience for the client, built into the steps. While your competition is relying on the same trusty (rhymes with rusty) selling steps, we will out play them and win. I will step you through the process of adding this layer of luxury experience. Plus I would like to uncover some missed opportunities that take your system to the next level or more. Again, I am not going to add or rename steps. Consider I am adding diamonds to the face and links of your fine timepiece.

For reference I listed on the next page the eight steps of the selling system I train. Then under the steps I referenced the book's **Luxury Experience** (L.E.) lessons we can apply and layer into these steps. Take the similar steps from your system and relate them to the sample.

Sample Selling System + L.E. Lessons

- **Prepare**
    - Choose Your Position
    - Create an Oasis
- **Welcome**
    - Create an Oasis
- **Create Need and Desire**
    - Make and Seize Opportunity
    - Serve and They Will Come
    - The Luxury Experience Client Book
    - A Luxury E-Mail Experience
    - Selling with the Power of Emotions
    - More Clients, More Often, Spending More Money
- **Present Product**
    - Harness the Power of Emotions
    - Building Value Above the Price
    - A Luxury E-Mail Experience
    - Success With Teamwork
- **Overcome Objections**
    - Harness the Power of Emotions
    - Building Value Above the Price
    - Success With Teamwork
    - Selling Against the Internet
- **Close**
    - Building Value Above the Price
    - Close on the Emotional High
    - Success With Teamwork
- **Add On**
    - Make and Seize Opportunity
    - The Luxury Service Client Book
    - Close on the Emotional High
    - More Clients, More Often, Spending More Money
- **Follow Up**
    - The Luxury Experience Client Book
    - A Luxury E-Mail Experience
    - Serve and They Will Come

CHOOSE YOUR POSITION

Did you see the news last night? How did it make you feel? If I had to guess, not well, right? We need to get out from underneath this black cloud and back to business without any delay.

Step one for you and your associates is to choose your position or attitude in today's climate. It is easy to listen to the news, other business people, or even a co-worker, and buy into the doomsday theory. Then you have an excuse for your reduced sales production and revenue. With this excuse you can get through the day, sleep well through the night and watch your business go under.

Self Fulfilled Prophecy

If it was not for bigger, excuse worthy news, weather has played an interesting role in sales. Have you ever heard an associate state "no one will be out to buy in this rain?" Then on a sunny day, "everyone will be at the lake today." Where's this associate's frame of mind when he does greet a client? How does this affect his coworkers?

No matter the source of dark clouds, don't let them hover over your place of business. And rather than being yet another self fulfilled prophecy let's get busy and make business happen.

Positive Response

When another business person or client asks "how's business," what do you answer? What ever the truth is, it should be something positive. It is not in your best interest to reveal downward sales trends or traffic counts to anyone but your business partners.

I was once interviewed by a local TV station during the 1990-91 Gulf War. They were doing a segment on how the war was affecting local retail business during the Christmas selling season. My business was holding its own with a modest increase over last year. But my answer to the press was; "Business is fantastic, I have sold many engagement and wedding rings to our armed forces hurrying off to get married before shipping out overseas". There was truth to this statement, and the message was quite the contrary to other interviews they made. That night my business had its 10 seconds of fame along with several others' 10 seconds of doom.

It's That Simple

It sounds so simple; "make the choice and business will happen." While this is just the first step, it is the core to all the rest. Without you and your staff's positive energy and drive, your clients experience would be mundane and quickly forgotten. It is not easy at times but with practice and a couple of successful experiences you will wonder, "Why did I waste so much time with a poor or negative position?"

So each morning when you get up and check the stock market over a cup of coffee, tell yourself; <u>today is filled with opportunities and I am excited to be part of the solution.</u> So go to work with that positive attitude and position then let it rub off on your co-workers and clients.

Key Points

- Watch the news but don't buy into the news.
- You and your competitors have to make the same decision on your position of the economy; you need to make the better choice.
- Don't look for a self-fulfilled prophecy or excuse.
- Carry a great attitude to work and share it with everyone.
- Spread the word that business is great using truthful facts. Leave out the bad news.
- Practice this decision making and relish in the rewards.

Manager's Notes

On any given day there could be an associate that chooses the wrong position. Don't let them infect the rest of the crew. Pull them aside and talk to them 1on1. Find out what might have caused this attitude and ask how you can help them. Let them know how important their choice is to the success of their and your business. Get a commitment for change and send them back out, or send them home until they can make the right choice.

If you find yourself in hot water you have three choices; one, be an egg and turn hard, two; be a carrot and turn soft, or three; be a coffee bean and change the water.

CREATE AN OASIS

Now that we have our minds focused in a positive, productive manner, we need to set the stage and atmosphere for our clients. What I am referring to is a recession free environment, an **Oasis** away from the everyday rat race. It takes more than a clean, organized and well lit store to create this environment. These things are important, but I assume they are already taken care of. And it is much more than positioning a greeter at the door to welcome your clients as they pass. (More on that subject later.)

My Oasis

We all have a place we go for relaxation, to clear our minds, or to take a much needed vacation. Think about your favorite place. Why is it we enjoy these locations? What do they offer that our everyday environment does not? Some would say simply a change of scenery. We need to take a closer look and make some observations.

Let me tell you about a newly discovered place my wife, Katie and I now enjoy. About an hour and a half drive from Portland Oregon is a lake called Lost Lake. We leave the freeway at the Town of Hood River, next to the Columbia Gorge. The drive from there is pleasant, with the road twisting through the tall evergreen trees. We pass freely through the opening to the lake and follow signs to the lodge. In front of us is a clear smooth lake reflecting the majestic trees outlining its shore. We walk the wide path and steps to the huge covered front porch of the log cabin lodge. While we sit at one of several picnic tables on the porch, we take in the sights, sounds and smells of this beautiful place. We don't know what we want to do first, but for some reason we are in no hurry.

There are boats to rent, good fishing and some excellent trails to hike. There are rooms on the top of the lodge, campsites for tents or trailers and rustic cabins to extend our stay. In the lodge we meet the shop keeper. He welcomes us to the lake and asks us "how was the drive?" I tell him excellent. Then he asks if this is our first visit, and we tell him it is. He lets us look around while he points out things of interest. Katie pours thru a photo album of other visitors experiencing the lake and resort. Our host points out some of the more interesting snapshots. I read a brochure on the facilities and give Katie a few highlights. We decide that we want to turn this day trip into a weekend.

We spent the two days kayaking in the motor free, crystal clear water, hiking the well maintained trails around the lake and enjoying each others company. The lake was unbelievable, so deep and clear you thought you were seeing a mile down. While kayaking, our paddles dipping in the water were the only sounds we heard until coming to a small stream of water falling over the rocks as it left the lake.

The trails were part dirt and natural pine needles. Then as needed they would elevate above the slanted terrain or soft marsh with built up wooden boardwalks. While walking one could not help but enjoy the smell of the trees and foliage surrounding you.

And best of all, the view of Oregon's tallest peak at 11,249', Mt Hood is on the horizon above us. I love to learn new things and a few years ago I took up snowboarding on Mt Hood. So a close up view of the mountain and its glaciers, also reflected in the mirror of the lake was very inspiring. We took lots of photos to share with our friends and preserve our memories.

A fly fisherman was floating in a raft as he hooked a large fish. Katie, I and several others watched as he worked for several minutes to land the trout. He paddled his boat to shore, towards the gathered crowd and stepped out into the shallow water. As the man and fish fought each end of the line we all shared in the excitement. Everyone was cheering him on. The fish was brought into the clear, one foot water and into the hands of the fisherman. He was a catch and release sportsman, so we had the pleasure of watching him care for the fish and watch it swim away. This story made it quickly to the lodge and campgrounds.

Pleasant conversations were exchange about the place with other happy visitors, but never once did we talk on a phone. The cell phone coverage ended a mile down the road. There are no TVs or newspaper stands and no public radio in the background. I can not remember seeing a clock on any walls and certainly no alarms next to our bed. We left Lost Lake with a renewed energy, inspiration and lots of memories to share.

Transplant the Oasis at Work

As you read that story I hope you forgot where you physically were or what else might have been on your mind. I know I was relaxed and absorbed in my surroundings and all that it had to offer. I forgot the rat race just a short drive away. If we could just bottle up this experience and let it pour out in our stores we would be the most popular place to shop. Maybe we can.

We aren't able to move mountain, lake or trees to our parking lot. But there are elements of the experience we can learn from. The objective is to put our guest's minds in a relaxed state and let them forget about the rat race they left.

OK, let's see how we can create a similar **Oasis** experience in our stores or offices for our clients. Using the above experience I will transplant some of the key attributes into our store.

Welcoming Impressions

The twisting drive thru the trees to the lake forced me to mentally slow down and enjoy the experience. While we can't control the traffic flow in our cities we do have some control over the experience in the parking lot. Are we and our employees parking at the far end so our guests get to park closer? Should we have a couple of spots marked for ten minutes or less? Are our products taking the best parking, as many car lots do? What if we teamed up with the other merchants in your shopping center and offered valet parking? *A Life Style Center I shop does this and a local auto dealership helps with sponsorship. They offer free valet for anyone driving their line. Some stores validate their guest's parking ticket. But even if the guest is paying three to five dollars it is perceived as a great service on a busy day.* Or if you see a client parking in the rain, have a big umbrella handy and meet them as they open their door. It can never be too early to make a first impression of your service.

From the time my wife and I drove into the lake park to the entry of the lodge we felt unobstructed and invited. While we don't have a national forest for an entrance and building a thirty foot front porch is out of the question, we can make improvements. Walk from your car to your front door today and take a critical look. Can you clearly see your place of business? Does it draw you in? Are the windows and doors clear of excessive signs or stickers? They should however see what type of business you are in without having to see your sign. The best way to communicate your business visually is with product displays in your windows.

As you walk the way to your door check that the paths are clear of unnecessary signs. Can we trim some shrubs or trees so guests can pass freely? Would a bench add some needed quick rest place and fit comfortably in your entrance? We want to alleviate our guests of any feeling of claustrophobia that they experienced elsewhere and get them to mentally slow down as they approach your door.

Open Spaces, Alluring Paths

Now is the time for our guest to open the door and walk across our lease line. There needs to be some decompression space between the entrance and the displays, signage and salespeople. We don't want products slapping them in the face during their first few steps or worse yet a salesperson standing at the doorway ready to pounce. Also a door greeter stationed there serves no purpose then to frighten clients like a bad Halloween skeleton. They should be able to walk in, take two or more steps and scan the store or office. They should see an inviting space, neat products well lit and tasteful decorations.

The visible staff should appear active but looking up at the newly arrived guest. Sales associates that are standing or sitting around watching the door are perceived as vultures ready to swoop. No one would want to enter when they see a group of waiting salespeople. Do not form groups or you could be perceived as a circling pack of wolves. Keep busy with cleaning, displaying stock, paperwork or making service calls. Try to do as much as you can on the customers side of the counters or displays. This will allow you to appear as a guest. And better yet, sales role-play with another associate or two as a customer, giving the guest the appearance of a busy store as they enter.

As the guest enters they should be greeted by the <u>nearest</u> associate available. We should never shout across another associate or the store. If we are across the store we are taking a few steps towards them without rushing. If we are all busy we still greet them and tell them we will be right with them. Be warm and don't forget to smile. And my favorite greeting is; "Welcome to *ABC Retailers.*" The word welcome says something we don't hear enough, not even in our own homes. Combine that with your business name and you have just planted your first sales seed.

Like the path thru the woods, the layout of the store should encourage browsing. Straight lines in shelves, displays, or counters remind us of the freeway lanes to be rushed through. Displays we can shop from both sides that have scattered or curved layouts create meandering. The more time a client spends in your place the more likely they will buy from you.

The wall hangings should show your products in use or some end result, inspirational so the clients can put themselves in the photo. If your products or services make their way into magazines or publications a rack of these publications should be displayed. You can tag the pages so the clients will easily find the items of interest. Or make up a photo album with clients and your products. These all become silent salespeople for you. Unless you sell clocks, take them down or relocate them out of view. We are in a time starved nation and we don't need any more reminders. I have witnessed clients bolting in the middle of a conversation when they see a clock.

Create a Tranquil Atmosphere

Now the store looks great and people are moving freely throughout. But how does it sound and smell? Are we making it comfortable and relaxing like a paddle on the lake? Or are there some distractions, more like public transportation?

We should have background music of a genre to fit our core client but somewhat on the more conservative side. And we should not use public radio. We do not want news, disc jockeys, weather or other advertisements broadcast in out stores and offices. I have heard more than once, direct competitor's ads playing in another one's store. XM commercial free radio works well and offers great program choices. A selection of CD's or a MP3 player would also do nicely. The idea is that you are in control and there will be no surprises to distract or confuse our guests.

Don't forget any TV screens. Play your choice of closed circuit programs and certainly not the news. Also it amazes me how many electronic stores I go into and see non working display models. Are they broke? If you have a screen, make sure it's working and in loop play mode.

Try to limit other sound distractions. IE; small tools, vacuum, loud phones, and nearby employee conversations. Also we should have our computer sound turned off. We could add a small water fountain in some stores to help soften outside noise.

A place of business should also be able to control the scent we would like our guest to smell. Out of all the human body's five senses, the sense of smell will retain the longest memory. If we are burning our lunch in the back of the store or always smell of some chemical, we would not register a luxury experience memory for our guests. Though, unless we are running a new age music store, most incense is out.

Check into some pleasant reed oil diffusers for a low maintenance solution. Some stores bake cookies or pop popcorn to give to their clients. This would then also be an unexpected treat. Just don't burn the food or more ground is lost. Also there are simply the plug-in air fresheners. What ever you choose, it should fit your core client's tastes. Pick only one scent and be consistent to embed a pleasant and persistent memory.

Wow Them Unexpectedly

OK, our guests are feeling pretty good. The space is inviting, the sounds and smells are pleasant, they feel relaxed and somewhat slowed down. Now let's exceed their expectations.

Like the walk around the lake; for no reason but our comfort the trail elevated above the slanted terrain and soft marsh with a built up wooden board walk.

What can be our board walk? We mentioned cookies or popcorn. You also could consider coffee or cold drinks. Or step it up with a cappuccino dispenser. *One very high-end company I know serves wine and mixed drinks using top shelf liquors. There is a single malt scotch served that becomes a great closing tool.* But you don't have to serve a lot of food and drinks to win over a client. Simple things; like a small tin of mints or bottled water with your business name imprinted sends a professional luxury experience message.

Every business seems to have some small service you can offer. Fine jewelry has the cleaning service, the tire business has flat repair, eye wear has clean and adjustments, and cosmetic counters give facials. These usually free services add to the luxury experience while leading to a new sale opportunity. What ever your products, consider a wellness check-up for anyone's like product. I saw this recently in a computer store. And I would love to have my car washed while I look over a new car. What ever services you choose, keep them simple and teach all staff members to provide these added perks.

Many of these services can be performed by one employee while another employee shows the guest around the store or office. Plus, it's a great way to slow the client down and get them to spend more time with you.

Memories to Share

Remember the story of the fisherman at the lake. That was a thrilling shared experience. In our stores our shared moment might be when we take a photo with our new client and their salesperson. We could send them a copy and add a copy to our album. Furthermore, when other guests see the camera flash go off they will want to share in the moment. Invite them over and build on the excitement as you hook your next fish.

Jumping to the final in-store impression; don't keep a physical barrier come between you and your guest. Come around and end each visit on their side of the counter or desk with your guest. Walk them to the door or carry the package to the car, if raining walk them with an umbrella. Shake their hand and sincerely thank them.

From the first impression to the last, you are building their experience today. You are creating memories, memories to be shared with their family, friends, and co-workers. Please make these luxurious.

Key Points

- Build your **Oasis** starting from the parking lot.
- Provide a clear, clean, and inviting physical and visual path to your office or storefront.
- Make sure your visual presentation communicates clearly of your business and products.
- Everyone needs some physical and mental space after walking in to decompress. Pull back the products, signs and sales people.
- Create an inspirational atmosphere with wall hangings, magazines and photos of your products in use or some end result.
- Eliminate the display of the waiting vultures, AKA, salespeople grouping or not doing anything.
- Eliminate distractions like clocks, public radio and TV.
- Declare a recession proof boundary around your store disallowing any negative communications.
- Encourage browsing with meandering displays.
- Bring the right sounds and scents to your **Oasis**.
- Exceed their expectations with an unexpected refreshment or small while-you-wait service.
- Whenever you can, create an experience that other guests can join and share.
- Allow each guest to leave with one final good impression, like a walk to the door and a sincere thank you.

Manager's Notes

There can be a lot of opportunity creating your **Oasis**. It will take some work to put yourself in your favorite place and discover why it makes you feel the way it does. Then it will need some thinking out of the box on how you can replicate those feelings in your place of business. Ask your staff about their getaways and for their ideas. Also ask some of your better clients, you might be surprised and how much they would like to help. And go shopping, pick the best known businesses in other product or service industry and see what they do to impress you. Also, check your direct competition and make sure they don't have one up on you.

Once you have decided as a group on what to do, spend plenty of time training and practicing new services with your staff. And be sure to make it a team environment. None of us are a one man band. Team up associates to provide these added services, pouring a drink or cleaning a ring, so the client never gets left alone. Throughout the book I will bring up other ways you and your associates will add to the atmosphere and guest experience.

Continue to watch your sales floor and participate often. Don't allow the vultures to gather. Encourage roll-plays and lead many of them yourself. Always be looking for more opportunities to improve your oasis.

Be prepared, when you start impressing your clients with a better environment and added services, they will tell their friends. Now you must consistently provide the same experience for their friends along with repeat visits from the current clients. Hold yourself and your associates accountable for every new and original **Service Standard**. Again use team work to provide an <u>unwavering</u> **Luxury Experience**. And enjoy the renewed popularity with your guests.

"Opportunity is missed by most people because it is dressed in overalls and looks like work."

— Thomas A. Edison

MAKE AND SEIZE OPPORTUNITY

Any of us that have been in sales for more than a few months have witnessed both easy times and slow times. During easy times everyone is doing well. You might have noticed less experienced salespeople doing as well as seasoned pros. Then when times are slow, have you noticed a few associates still doing well while most others are not making their goals? I have seen this time and time again.

A true professional will take advantage of their opportunities. Any time a guest walks thru the door there is opportunity. Let's take a look at what we can learn from the differences between up and down associates and the steady professionals.

The Clerk

When there is plenty of business to go around many of us become what I call clerks. We greet the guest, help them find what they are looking for and ring up the sale. If we get resistance to buy we move on to the next customer. As long as there is always another guest walking in the door for the clerks, business happens, but when the traffic slows so does their production. This steady stream of customers ready and willing to buy are becoming few and far between.

I can often visit a store and easily spot this clerk type salesperson. They are usually the ones waiting close to the door for their next sale. They are not busy with their client book or writing thank you notes. They are the first to welcome you though. This is how they try to survive, greet more walk-ins to increase their chance of sales success. Then once they have a client to help, they often rush through the process, even skip steps of the sale and miss opportunities to either make the sale today or build opportunity for tomorrow. The reason I find that they rush the sales process is they are worried to miss out on an easier sold or larger ticket customer. They actually want to get back to waiting at the door for their imaginary friend. This type of salesperson can be quick to judge or size up a client on their ability or willingness to buy. Plus they are often looking only for a sale today and see no value in planting seeds for tomorrow's business.

Another large mistake made by clerks is to help the client only as asked. Allow me give you an example.

A guest comes in for a battery change on a watch; they are greeted at the front door by an eager clerk. The clerk takes the watch to the back, leaving the guest to browse. After changing the battery the clerk has the cashier ring up the sale, not wanting to waste any more time with a ten dollar service. He or she then returns to the waiting spot at the front door hoping for more on the next opportunity.

The guest did leave with a working watch, but wasn't there something missing in their experience? The clerk had very little interaction with this guest, the cashier may have captured their name in the computer but no other personal connection was made.

The Sales Professional

The sales professional should be doing everything possible to not only make a sale but to maximize the potential opportunities as well. I will use the same scenario of the guest coming in for a watch battery replacement and uncover as many opportunities the clerk missed. As the new scenario unfolds, additional opportunities will present themselves and the true professional will seize these as well. Also, imagine the guest's experience as you read this story.

As the guest walks in the door he sees several busy associates, and then is greeted by a salesperson as she puts aside glass cleaning tools. After welcoming him to the store the saleslady introduces herself to him and asks him for his name.

After explaining he is in only for a watch battery replacement the saleslady compliments him on his watch and assures him it will be taken care of promptly. She then calls over another associate to assist with the battery replacement. While the second associate takes the watch to the back room, the saleslady offers and pours the client a drink.

They start a conversation of when and how he obtained his watch. She leads him over to the watch showcase, promising to show him something special. She pulls from the case an 18kt gold watch with a diamond dial and bezel, and smoothly clasps it on his empty wrist. This timepiece is fifty times more expensive than the guest's current watch, he is blown away. This then leads to a conversation of how he has always dreamed of owning a fine timepiece such as this. The saleslady explains the value in the product and builds on the prestige of its ownership. The client brags a little about a recent promotion at work and how this would be a symbol of his accomplishment. And they talked together about his business.

By this time both the saleslady and the client are laughing and having a good time, and the client was still wearing the new watch. When the saleslady asked her client how many links she should remove, he replied "two should be perfect". With the clients credit card in her hand she turned the conversation to his wife. She then pulled out the lady's version of his new timepiece. He explained that she would never wear a watch, but that she did want bigger diamond earrings. They found the perfect pair of studs about the same price as his watch.

The saleslady also showed him a matching diamond necklace and bracelet. He asked her to keep them on a wish list for later. As they wrote up a client profile page together, the second associate sized the new timepiece and gift boxed the diamond earrings.

The client left with his old watch in the box, proudly wearing his new timepiece. Plus he was very excited to present his wife with her beautiful diamond studs and looked forward to a long relationship with his newfound sales professional.

What Went Right

The above scenario was taken from a true story. Now, not every time does a ten dollar service turn out to be a several thousand dollar sale. But even without the client buying, his experience would have been much better than in the first example. Let's look at the breakdown of what went right to lead to this positive experience and sales success.

#1, the store's associates were busy, there were no vultures waiting to swoop.
#2, the greeting was warm and professional, using names and compliments.

#3, our associate asked for assistance from a second salesperson. The guest was not left alone.

#4, a drink was offered and accepted. Then a conversation was started by the associate.

#5, the client was led to a sales counter with a promise of something special.

#6, our guest was flattered and excited with the presentation and trying on of a fabulous product.

#7, the saleslady has a no fear attitude with showing and selling an expensive item. She did not pre-judge.

#8, the guest feels comfortable to talk about his business accomplishments. Then the saleslady builds the value of the product based on the guest's emotions.

#9, while they are talking, the associate has our guest wear the timepiece, creating comfort of ownership.

#10, our saleslady uses a non-threatening assumption close with the band sizing question.

#11, the credit card was collected, closing the deal on the watch. Then our superstar kept selling, never leaving the guest.

#12, a client page was filled out with wish list items added.

Wow! A lot of great things came together to make a successful, luxury experience. Numbers 1, 2, and 4, have been discussed in previous chapters. Numbers 3, 8, 10, and 12; I will discuss in following chapters. So, we should take a closer look at the rest. Outlined below are the elements that can help turn an ordinary store visit into a luxury experience, and lead to more business.

Flatter and Excite All Guests

All guests in our place of business should be shown a product. This seems so rudimental, but every day you can see many examples of this not happening. Common excuses I hear are; "he was just in for a service," "they were just looking," "we did not have what they were looking for," "they weren't here to buy," and "they did not ask to see anything."

If I were to ask these guests not shown products, after leaving, here's what they would probably say; "they were too lazy," "they pre-judged me," "I was ignored," "they did not want to be bothered," "I was afraid to ask," or "they were snobby." I would not want to hear any of these excuses from my associates any more than these comments from my guests.

Would you like to read more on how we can be perceived? Google "snobby sales associate" or "rude..." I bet you can find some well known and some well deserved stores on this search list. I hope though, you are not listed.

In-order to fatter and excite all guests I would like to introduce to you to a process used in many luxury stores. I call it **Dazzle**. **Dazzle** is the simple act of sharing with your guest one of your most expensive or impressive products. When you share such an item with the guest it will flatter and excite them.

You should always have your favorite products in mind and handy for your guests. Choose some of the most expensive items in your store in each category for these **Dazzle** items. Sometimes it is a shot in the dark if this is something they will like or have an interest in. But it is not our objective to necessarily sell the most expensive product. What we are accomplishing is flattering our guest with the assumption that they would like it and can afford it.

There are a couple ways we can achieve the simple task of getting **Dazzle** products in the hands of our guests. One is to say, "Before you go there is something I want to share with you." Then either go get the promised product if they are occupied, or bring them to the product. Use this with a service counter guest and the "just looking" guest. Always put the product in their hands, on their body, or sit them in it, depending on the product of course. The other method is to silently bring the product to the guest, then announce you have something special to share with them.

Dazzle can break the ice and lead to a conversation about what they would like. It is always best practice to start high and work in that price range till there is a valid objection that we can not overcome. Then step down, slowly. Everything else will seem even more affordable. Do not try to pre-judge and share a less expensive item to some.

*I once had a one million dollar bracelet to **Dazzle** my guests. The word got out and people came with hopes to also try it on. Then I heard of one guest telling a friend that they were not chosen, or worthy of being shown this product.* Be consistent, everyone is worthy.

Always allow them to hold, touch, wear or sit on the **Dazzle** product. If you don't we will lose the flattering effect. <u>As long as we hold onto the product we are sending the message that we own it and they can not afford it.</u> <u>Only when they have it in their hands does the mental transfer of ownership take place.</u> With this mental transfer of ownership comes the feeling of excitement.

Also let them keep possession of the product as long as they wish. If you ask for it back you will end the sales process without a sale. If they hand it back right away, it shows little interest. Then start asking questions to find out why, and what they would like. But the longer they hold or wear it the more interest they have in it. Watch their body language and eye movements. If they are looking at the product as you talk, they are more interested, keep selling. If they are looking at the walkway to the backroom, they want their old watch back and could be a little nervous. You might have to back down some with your sales pitch.

I have often heard guests say that I have just made their day when I **Dazzle** them. Think about that; you can be the highlight of a guest's day with a simple act. Whether it is sitting in a top of the line sports car, trying on a diamond bracelet, or listening to a high-end home entertainment system; they are going to be impressed, and the thought of ownership will enter their mind.

Never Stop Selling

Our saleslady took her client from a ten dollar service, to showing and selling a very expensive timepiece. She did this with no fear. The worse that could have happened is that he handed the timepiece right back to her and said no thanks. But then their conversation would continue, and maybe lead to some other item of interest. Or he might have left with only his old watch on his wrist. However, you can be sure that when he went home to his wife, or back to work with his peers, he told them about wearing the timepiece. His peers could be in for the same experience or his wife to purchase what excited him. And don't forget the wish list on the client page the sales associate has now. Opportunities, made from a single guest with a ten dollar service.

And then, she never stopped selling. Even the seasoned pros can become clerks the moment they have the client's credit card in their hands. They would rush it to the cashier and disappear in the backroom to personally size his new watch band. The client would be happy, sucking ice cubes dry as he waited, alone. But instead, using the excitement of his self purchase, she led into an easy add-on item for his wife. The "clerk" associate would want to quickly wrap up the watch to get back on the floor for their next opportunity.

The fact of the matter is; <u>the client you just sold is today's most qualified, best hope for a second sale, today!</u> You just won them over, they trust you, and they are on an emotional high. You can tap into this opportunity before it goes dry like the ice cubes. Never leave your guest alone, have someone assist with the sizing and boxing. Get to know them better, refill their drink, write up that wish list and client profile sheet, and add-on!

Once, my assistant manager turned over a man and his wife to me. He was buying her a strand of pearls. My assistant told me the man was grumpy, but I paid it no attention. As my assistant was boxing the strand of pearls, I introduced myself and told them I wanted to show them something special while they waited. I came around to their side of the counter, told her to close her eyes and hold out her arm. I clasped my most expensive diamond bracelet on her wrist. She was flattered and thrilled. Her husband could not help but notice her excitement and barked "will that shut you up for awhile?" In less than two minutes we increased that ticket amount over five times. And the grumpy man did smile and laugh as his wife left with both pieces.

In later chapters we will discuss how teamwork can help make a difference too. But it's the no fear, show high and never stop selling attitude that makes things happen.

Key Points

- You must take full advantage of every guest coming into your store, whether for a service or just browsing.
- Don't be a clerk; waiting for that rare "I'd like to buy…" customer. Also, please don't help a guest only as they ask. Go the extra steps to make (more) business happen.
- Have **Dazzle** products ready to show. Pick your best and most expensive items that will impress everyone.
- Use a statement like "before you go there is something special I am going to show you." Don't ask if they want to see it, just bring them to it or it to them.
- Always put the product on them, them in it, or let them hold it. This transfers mental ownership and tells them that they can buy it. If you hold it, it sends the message that they can not afford it. Then let them possess it as long as they like. Watch their body language.
- Have a no fear attitude. Show high will sell high. Then you can step down if needed, slowly.
- Do not pre-judge with the **Dazzle** process or anytime you sell.
- Use **Dazzle** as an icebreaker with "just lookers." Never let a guest leave without holding at least one fantastic product. Make the visit the highlight of their day.
- Never leave your guest alone. You or another sales associate should be with your guest at all times to increase the opportunity to sell.
- Never stop selling. The best prospect of the day is the client that just agreed to make a purchase. Keep your guest on his emotional high and sell him again. It is easier to sell the second item then the first in most instances.

Manager's Notes

As you read this chapter you will identify the good and bad behaviors in your associate's, corresponding to this lesson. You know where, and with whom, your challenges and opportunities lie. Put a stop to clerk behaviors in your store.

Teach and practice the techniques. Then spend lots of time following up on the sales floor. Make certain we **Dazzle** every guest. Do not accept excuses from your associates.

Some have said it takes a month of days to form a new habit. What I have found is that it takes only the will to change and the decision to just do it. You may have heard of the simple "Will or Skill" behavior change management question. ("Why doesn't Bruce **Dazzle** every guest? Is it will or skill?") We can teach each other the skill, and then we just need to have the will to do it. And choose to do it.

Share many success stories to flatter and excite your team.

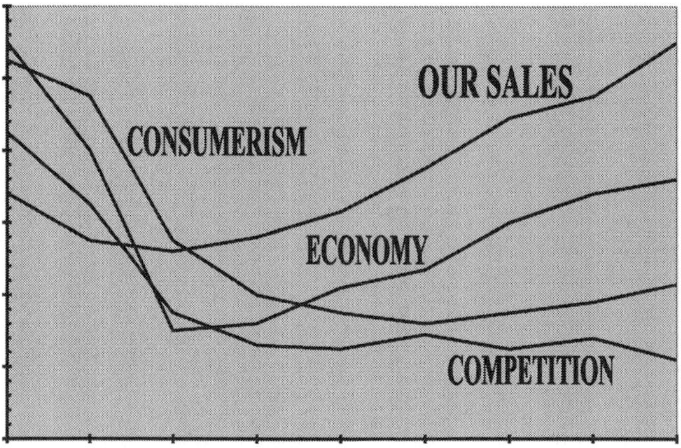
OUR SALES
CONSUMERISM
ECONOMY
COMPETITION

SERVE AND THEY WILL COME

You might be blessed with all the walk-in traffic you need or want. If so, you could skip this chapter. But if your door is not swinging open continuously then this chapter should be helpful.

Another thing to consider is the type of traffic you receive. Are the guests your core client or are they truly just lookers? While we want all types of traffic, we do desire as many qualified buyers as possible.

Our Competition

One point you should keep in mind for your business; everyone is your competition for the same consumer dollar. Jewelers compete with handbags and shoes, car dealers encounter losses with, home re-modelers, and home entertainment contends against the travel industry. The list goes on and travels in a complete interconnected circle. In our selling we must be prepared to promote our products and services against all our competitors.

We have control of how our clients remember us (and our store) through our interaction with them. The services we provide and our commitment to their personal needs creates an experience. They will remember the experiences they have with us and desire more, more than any other competitor.

Promote From Within

We can not rely just on advertising to bring us the clients we need. In-fact when business is down, one of the first cuts we see in many budgets is marketing. We as salespeople and managers need to do all we can inside our four walls to promote our business. And we can do this much more effectively than any form of mass advertising. Plus advertising does not always bring in the best qualified consumer. As I have said; it is much easier to sell the same client a second time then to win over a new client. Then if we keep our current clients happy they will refer their friends, family and neighbors, again much easier to sell then a stranger.

Allow me to outline a client service program to help bring back your most qualified prospects.

The Luxury Experience Service Call

Step one, select a luxury service. From the products you sell, pick a service that you and your staff do or could do as a service for free. IE; jewelry cleaning and gemstone inspection, battery change in a watch (before it dies), oil change on a car, program upgrade on a computer, how to lesson on a camera, wax on a snowboard, wellness check on a laptop, insurance replacement value update on a valuable, wash and vacuum of auto, winterize a boat, safety check brakes and tires on a motorcycle, or a soon to expire warranty service check on any item. Do not pick anything you would have to charge your guest even the smallest amount. It is key that it be something you can do while they wait and provide a needed service. I have found the "soon to expire warranty service check" to be well received with my clients, yet have found no one else doing such a service. Let's use this service as the example for the rest of the steps.

Step two, access your purchase history database. Run a sales history report for a given product brand or category. Knowing the warranty period, say one year, print this report for nine months ago. Sort them out for each sales associate if applicable and possible. I believe it is always best to let the sales associate build the relationship with their guests, plus they are better able to connect with their clients. When you first start this service program you might have several months of sales to catch up on. After catching up do a month at a time each new month. So with a one year warranty; you would be listing clients, sold in January, on October 1st and so forth. Do this with all your product lines.

Step three, develop a call procedure and script. I have found only phone calls to give the needed success. Direct mail will get lost in all the rest of the junk offers. An E-Mail might give a lead-in to the call but then the call is still needed to bring the guest into the store. More on E-Mail in a later chapter but I'll stick to a calling campaign for this service. We must keep the call to benefit the guest only. It is not a call to sell a new product or an extended warranty. Our objective is to bring our guests back into our store and to let them know we care about their satisfaction of the product we sold them. Be prepared to make a personal connection with your client. Have their complete purchase history and their client profile sheet in front of you. (More on client profile books in the next chapter.) You want to be able to ask "how did Jill's soccer tournament go?" or "did Bobby like his new computer?" Be equipped to answer questions on more than just the product you are calling about. Make an appointment with them for your service. Have your work schedule handy so you can personally serve them. Then they will also feel more committed to come in and keep this personal appointment.

So the call could go like this; "*Hi Tom, this is Bruce from ABC Retails. I am calling about the widget I sold you last January. How are you today?* I'm fine, what's up Bruce? *Well, I want to make sure you are pleased with the widget, it has a one year warranty and I would like to give it a wellness service check before the warranty is up. The service, along with any needed repair, is free to you. I would do the wellness check while you wait.* OK, sounds good. What do I need to do? *Can you bring it by after work tomorrow, say 5:00 O'clock? I will make sure I am free to help you.* No problem, I will see you then. *Great, hey Tom, how did Jill's soccer tournament go?* They won and now on to State, thanks for asking, your memory is amazing. *Thanks, I bet she is excited. So I will see you tomorrow night.* Yes, thanks Bruce, see you tomorrow."

I like to get to the point of the conversation right away, even before asking how they are doing. They know you are not calling to make small talk. And if you were to ask about Jill's soccer before getting to business it would just seem like a lead-in to the sales pitch. Once they realize you are not calling to sell them something then they are much more relaxed. Also, I do not like the question "have I reached you at a good time?" The honest answer to that question at all times is NO. Plus it just makes us all irritable that you are not getting to the point.

As I was writing this paragraph, my doorbell rang, my dogs went tearing thru the house barking, I got up and opened the door to a door-to-door salesperson. With clip board in hand the young salesperson complimented me on a recent porch remodel and asked me a couple questions about it, all while one dog was squirming in my arms growling at the person and the other barking behind me. I clearly did not want to small talk my way to the sales pitch. Assume the same when you call on the phone. But if you are brief, to the point, offering only a service and connect on a personal level this call can be very positive.

Step four, now prepare for their visit. Be ready to perform the service as promised. Team up with another associate to help with the service while you stay with the guest. And double check that the **Oasis** stage is set. Have all the same information, purchase history and client profile sheet handy. Do further research and shopping for them. What's on their wish list? What products would compliment their past purchases, who else in their family need your products or what is new inventory since they have been in last?

Step five, enjoy the visit. When the guest arrives get someone right onto the service. *(Hint; prearrange with all services that the client's serviced product is not brought back to you or your client until requested by you. One, we don't want to interrupt a sales presentation at any time. And two, we would like the guest to stay in our store as long as possible. It is up to the salesperson to watch their guest's body language and signals so they don't feel uncomfortable or held hostage at any time.)* Provide your guest with a drink or snack if available. Now is a good time to make some personal small talk, but tell them that you have something to show them before they go. Lead them to the products of interest. Show them something new. Flatter them with a demo of the most expensive product. Watch for buying signals or peaked interest and react to them. Make it easy for them to make a decision to buy, but don't try to hard close your good client. Make sure you are both having fun and laughing. Use this time to update their wish list. Ask them about any special occasions they have in the future.

When done right, these steps will provide a level of service not offered by many businesses. It will bring your clients in when they had no plans to come in. And it will give you twice the chance of selling something then the next stranger walking into the store on this same night. You have nothing to loose and everything to gain. Even if the client does not buy he will remember the service, tell his friends and co-workers and then also come back when he is ready to buy.

Key Points

- We always need more and better qualified buying traffic.
- Our current clients are our best source for this traffic.
- We must keep our current clients happy even when they have no intention of another purchase, yet.
- This is a created opportunity with a greater chance of sales success then the stranger you are hoping will walk in the door right now.
- Service beyond what is expected will produce sales and referrals.
- Having a list of added services after the sale will create a habit with our guests to return to us.
- These services must be free and while you wait, and shop.
- Use your purchase history database to seek out and organize the call list.
- The most effective way to reach out to our guests to offer these services is with a well planned, timely "service only" call.
- We must team-up with our associates to provide the service while we stay with our guest.
- This is an opportunity to impress and flatter your clients. They will feel special and appreciated. **Dazzle** them.
- We must use every face to face opportunity with our guests to nurture a relationship, create desire for our products and provide a needed service.
- Don't forget to keep the **Oasis** "green".

Manager's Notes

The challenge you face with this sort of objective and assignment is associate buy-in and execution. Most retail salespeople hate to use the phones; they are not "telemarketers". Look right now onto your sales floor. Is everyone busy? Or are a few waiting for someone to walk in and hand them money? Remember the **Oasis**, no vultures waiting to swoop. We have the time, I have outlined some of the benefits, and you can provide the motivation and training to see that it gets done. Be organized with the client call lists. Ask that associates keep call records and results on these lists and hand them back to you. Like any project, monitor it closely and look for success stories. It won't be just like my example, some calls will lead right to a sale then some times we will get nowhere. Share the success stories and learn from the others.

As you complete the meetings and trainings of this chapter and others, you will be collecting a list of experiences and services your guests should encounter. Take a look at chapter lesson "Create Your Culture and Live Your Dream." Your lessons now and throughout the book will develop into your company's service standards that all guests need to experience.

THE LUXURY EXPERIENCE CLIENT BOOK

If I were to interview the top salesperson from 100 different business what two things make them successful, I would have 100 different answers for the first and all the same for the second. Every salesperson has their unique sales pitch, closing line, guest service, add-on technique, and so forth. But they would all have to agree; customer follow-up and client cultivating is what put them on top. Ask any personal shopper in your favorite upper-end department store. Their follow up system, a client book earned them that position. You can expect to increase your business by 30 to 50 percent with proper use of a client book and clienteling.

In this day and age of computers I assume you have a database full of your clients' names, addresses, phone numbers and e-mail boxes. This is great, and needed to maintain purchase history and such. It can also be invaluable for direct mail and e-mail marketing. In the last chapter I instructed to use this database to access purchasers by branded product and dates of purchase. You can not replace the computer for a fact storage and retrieval device. But I do not know as of yet a computer program that can replace the properly organized and religiously used client book of a successful salesperson. Features that set the day planner sized client book above the computer are; accessibility, it is available throughout the store and always on and ready for data entry or retrieval, effortlessness, anyone can write a few simple lines, adaptable, we can create new fields of data with the swipe of a pen, personable,... OK, you get the idea. (But did I mention dependable?)

I wish to cover the basic elements of a typical client book, give basic instructions on how to use it, and add the layer of luxury to make it more successful. On the next two pages is the front and back of the client profile page of my **Luxury Experience Client Book System**. This page is the heart of the guest follow-up and client cultivation process.

PERSONAL SERVICE RECORD

Name _____ **Birthday** _____

Spouse _____ **Aniv.** _____ **Birthday** _____

Address ☐ _____

City _____ **State** _____ **Zip** _____

Phone Hm ☐ _____ **Cell** ☐ _____

Phone Wk ☐ _____ **Spouse** ☐ _____

E-Mail ☐ _____

Check Preferred Contact Method and Address.

Business _____

Address ☐ _____

Other Info _____

_____

_____

Salesperson _____ Date _____

Items of Interest   Price

_____   _____   _____

_____   _____   _____

_____   _____   _____

_____   _____   _____

_____   _____   _____

Occasion _____ Date _____

Notes _____

_____

_____

Purchase History:

Date	Items	TY	SC	SC	SC
_____	_____	___	___	___	___
_____	_____	___	___	___	___
_____	_____	___	___	___	___
_____	_____	___	___	___	___
_____	_____	___	___	___	___
_____	_____	___	___	___	___
_____	_____	___	___	___	___
_____	_____	___	___	___	___
_____	_____	___	___	___	___
_____	_____	___	___	___	___
_____	_____	___	___	___	___

Follow-Up:

Guest Services:

Date	Service	Result
_____	_____	_____
_____	_____	_____
_____	_____	_____
_____	_____	_____
_____	_____	_____
_____	_____	_____
_____	_____	_____
_____	_____	_____
_____	_____	_____

The **Personal Service Record** sheet is just that, a place to record the personal service that you will give to your client in-order to win them over for life. When used correctly you will earn their business, exceed their expectations, and receive their referrals. Let me walk you through how to use this sheet.

Guest Information

The first step is to gather your guest's information. This is started with the first contact, whether by phone, e-mail or in person. Having the blank sheets handy at the phone, service and sales counter is needed.

As you talk to the guest start writing notes and filling in the sheet's fields. If you are in-front of the guest you can explain the form and how it will help you both. *("Don, I want to make sure I don't miss any details so I am taking some notes that we will use throughout our business together, and if I am off anytime you are back in anyone can look up our notes.")*

Some associates have found success giving the client the form to fill out the top half. I have labeled this part bold and laid it out in a familiar format. You might be surprised how much more information they are willing to write as apposed to being asked each one of these questions, like birthday, anniversary, or phone numbers.

Treat all this information with secure confidentiality. Also note a check mark of preferred method of contact. Knowing the direct and best way to reach your client is vital. You would hate to be the one to surprise a spouse before the occasion. I have seen a few sales lost and clients upset with this "small" mistake.

"Other info" includes but not limited to; children's names and birthdays, hobbies or other interests, drink preference from your **"Oasis** bar", life events coming up or their favorite sports teams. Anything that will help you make a connection and serve your guest. You would fill this out as you get to know your guest in conversations.

Items of Interest

The "Items of Interest" is their wish list. Hopefully you have sold them something today and you can record that on the back of the form. The wish list is created by asking questions. "What would you like next?" And follow up with "what is your one big dream item?" Now you have two for the list.

Of course you should be showing these products to your guest and using your best salesmanship to make them attainable today. But if they remain on the wish list it would be a good time to inquire about any upcoming occasions to celebrate with these items, or if you have their permission, contact their spouse and help them with the items as a gift.

Other Notes

The rest of the front page is completed by you as you help your guest shop or as soon as they leave. Salesperson is you and a team member if involved. Date of first visit is helpful. Be sure to make note of you SKU or stock number, product or service and retail price plus discounts if any. On the occasion line jot down why they were shopping. As you fill in multiple items of interest the occasion could be noted on each line item. Other notes should be things like finger, shoe, dress sizes, special requests, delivery time quoted and so forth.

A Bird in the Hand…

A word of caution, the completion of even the best client profile sheet does not put food on the table. I have seen cases where the store's lowest producing associate had a book full of completed sheets. I found that this salesperson was a poor closer and needed more training in this area.

Do not forget your steps to the sale, use the client sheet as a tool to help you thru these steps, not as a crutch to skip any steps including closing the sale on their first visit. As you may have heard, "there is no such thing as a be-back." I believe there is merit in that statement, so close your sale today if at all possible. Then use the client sheet to create the next sale to your client.

Purchase History and Follow-Up

Now onto the back page for follow-up… Use your computer to help keep the purchase history updated accurately. I recommend that at the end of each month you print out a list of sales you made for the month. This list should be by sales associate and include the client's name. Then the associate can make sure they have a client page and follow-up with the guest. Having this information in your book and at your finger tips will be useful later.

Take a look at the back page, "TY" is Thank You. Without a doubt you will make a lasting impression and build personal loyalty if you write and send timely thank you notes. These notes should be hand written on a simple greeting style card. (E-mail can also be used if that is the guests preferred method of contact. See the next chapter on hints to get the most out of e-mail along with these instructions for a "snail-mail" card.)

Numerous successful businesses have cards printed with the company logo embossed on the cover and blank on the inside so they can be used for other purposes also.

Keep the note simple and personal. Do not use this note to try and sell something else, just thank them for their business and wish them many years of enjoyment. I have even found the inclusion of your business card a less then subtle hint for more business, so refrain away from it too.

Many organized associates will write the thank you card as soon as the client leaves. You can wait a couple days to mail, but then it is written before you forget. Be sure not to endanger confidentiality or ruin a surprise. Use the preferred address and know the reason for the purchase. I put the safe mail date in small print where it is covered by the postage stamp later.

Cards should also be sent after a first visit to your business, even when they don't purchase. Send these right way, they will still be in the purchasing mode and come back. If you find thru a follow-up call they have chosen not to purchase, you could still send them a card thanking them for the opportunity. They will be more likely to give you another chance later.

One more important thank you card is needed when a client refers another to you. Send the referring client a card whether or not the referral buys. Some associates or business have a gift program for referrals. I have more on that in a later lesson. Another deserving reason for a TY note is when a client pays you a compliment. This could be in casual conversation to another client, or a written note to you boss. Record the date you mailed the cards under TY for a purchase thank you. See Guest Services for recording others.

"SC" stands for Service Call. These are phone calls, or e-mails if appropriate, that you have made in regards to the product sold. A good reason for a call is to check on how they are doing with the new product. Don't assume if you don't hear from them they are happy. Be proactive; calling them is so much better than them calling you with a problem. You might uncover a concern, but handling it proactively will further your relationship with you client.

A good time to call would be from 5 to 10 days after the sale, if a self purchase. Or if a gift, call at the office the next business day after the occasion. (I say at the office because sometimes gifting plans change.) This too is not a good time to try selling further unless they lead you into the conversation. This call should only replace the thank you card if the guest has not given you permission to mail or e-mail. Other call reasons would come from the previous chapter. Keep the dates recorded.

Guest Services

The last part of the form is "Guest Services". This space is used for recording contacts with your clients about future sales, events and services. I could have named this clienteling, or client cultivating. I didn't simply because these forms are seen by our clients at times and I don't want them to think we are going to hound them. In fact, that is the last thing we would want to do. <u>If every call, e-mail or card has the guests best interest in mind we will be more successful and never perceived pushy.</u> In years of shopping and buying many products I have only felt over called once or twice. And even then I was not angry in the least. The truth is 99 out of 100 times I received no follow-up and many times it would have been warranted.

Most sales people do not follow-up after a customer steps out of the store, with a purchase or not. We assume the guest does not want to hear from us, this is not so. We think we would be too pushy to call, not true. We are afraid of rejection, and sometimes that can happen. What is the worst that can happen; that they tell you no thanks.

Just today I made a call to a client I had been putting off. I expected them to contact me a few days ago, and when they didn't I thought they had changed their mind to use my services. I did not want to be rejected. I even thought," how rude not to at least let me know so I can remove them from my appointment calendar." When I called today she was glad I called. Then we picked up right where we had planned on our last meeting and look forward to mutual success together.

People live busy lives, they need help making decisions and keeping appointments. We all put things on the back burner or even forget. It is our job to help them remember and to make their decisions easy. So get over the fear of rejection or being perceived as pushy and use reasons throughout this book to make contact with your clients. Then record these contacts and results on their "Personal Service Record" sheet.

Now that you have some fantastic client sheets we need to keep them organized and manage our follow-up system. The rest of the client book and its layout are designed to do just that. Keep it simple and clean so anyone could find a client page if needed. This will earn you a sale or two on your days off.

Alpha Tabs and Follow-Up Pending

You should have a set of alpha tabs to file most of your client sheets. Then for only the current, sale pending client sheets have a tab for "follow-up needed" or "pending action". Keep these cleaned out and move them to the alpha file when no action is needed right away. Try to keep your client sheets organized under these two tabbed locations only. Don't make it hard for you or a teammate to find a needed sheet. An exception is when the book becomes full. Many successful salespeople will have multiple planner sized binders to alphabetize their client pages. Just keep them all on the same shelf with your current planner.

Planning Calendar and Delivery Log

You should have a planning calendar in your book. Use this to record needed follow-up with all clients, to record delivery promised dates and other actions and events. You must be looking at this daily and always scan ahead. <u>Be proactive and solve any issue before the guest has to call you.</u>

Any time you have promised to contact a guest, keep you promise. Even if you do not have the information or answer, just call and let them know you are still working on it. This will go along ways to earn your clients confidence and loyalty. <u>Always under promise and over deliver with everything you do.</u>

Keep another log for special orders, service and repairs for your guests. Even if this log is kept in the office, you should also keep a log for your clients. If you take the <u>personal responsibility</u> that your client's goods and services are delivered on time (or sooner) <u>you will overcome a large source of customer complaints in the retail industry</u>. I have included a sample of this delivery log on a proceeding page.

Life Events

Another section in the book is tabbed with the months of the year. Behind each of these tabs is a simple log of your guests' life events and occasions. You should record birthdays of theirs, spouses and family members, anniversaries, graduations, retirements, baby due dates, or any other occasion that warrants a contact from you.

You will want to be using this one month ahead to send cards, e-mails and make calls. Most of these events will be reoccurring yearly, but if not cross them off when done. Use as many forms behind each month tab as needed and keep them current.

Once you have this simple systems in place don't let it slip. If you were to send birthday, anniversary and holiday cards for a few years then forget one year, it would not go unnoticed.

I will never forget a good client of mine and how he perceived this system. I sent him and his wife birthday, anniversary and holiday cards. His wife would be sure to display the card from me proudly on the kitchen table. He would then come to see me within a day or two and purchase something off his wife's wish list. He always told me I was his best reminder service of gift giving events. After a couple years he even offered me the opportunity to manage a business he just purchased. And he said it was all from my client follow-up and services. Again, I have a sample page of this form included.

Sales Goals and More

I believe you should have a page or two of your personal sales dollar numbers in your client book. This outline or spread sheet should be for the current year, comparing last year, and broken down by month. A second page could show your daily sales for the current month. They both need to show your sales goals compared to the actual results.

Though this has nothing to do with your clients' experience, it is important for you and your business to keep this handy and a focus of why we are doing these added benefits. Plus it is a good way of tracking the results of you extra efforts. See a sample of these pages at the end of this chapter.

Many client books could include other tabs or sections, IE: Company Mission Statement, Service Standards List, Product Knowledge References, Steps to a Sale System, Procedure Cheat Sheet, Training Check List, Blank Guest Profile Sheets, Blank Sales Slips, Service Forms, Credit Application, Price Lists, Note Pad, Pen, or even small tools. Just don't make it too cluttered or heavy that you won't want to carry it.

This chapter covers a lot of information but if you apply all this information it will take your sales performance to the next level or more. I expect new sales associates to see small results after the first month and large results after the first year. It is not just for the long term resident pro. Start with the basics and develop your own additions of services and procedures you do using your **Luxury Experience Client Book**.

Key Points

- The Client Book is for the benefit of the customer and the proper use of it will enhance the **Luxury Experience** we provide for our guests.
- You should expect increased results after just your first month and 30 to 50 percent increase in your personal sales the second year by using the Client Book.
- You must keep you Client Book complete, accessible, organized, and current.
- Record guests' information completely and gain permission to contact them in their preferred method.
- Learn more about your guests including life event dates and other interests.
- Use personal notes to reconnect with your clients now and later.
- DO NOT use the completion of the client page as a crutch to skip steps of the sales process. Close the sale today, clientele tomorrow.
- Use thank you notes for first visits, purchases, referrals and paid compliments that come back to you.
- Record all follow-up and service contacts.
- Use the Calendar and Delivery Log to keep all promises.
- Be organized and consistent with all monthly occasion cards.
- Add to your book information and tools to make it a useful reference at the sales counter.

Manager's Notes

One of the biggest challenges with many associates is with them not getting the guest's information, or a completely filled out client sheet. Sometimes they are afraid to ask for the information. Other times it can be the wrong approach with the guest. We do need to gain the guest's confidence in us before they would release personal information. This takes some time with them on the sales floor building rapport. But before a guest leaves we should have some customer benefiting reason to contact them later, like a special price quote, another product choice, or to send some more product information. The reason to collect the information and to follow-up with the guest must be presented to the guest. And these reasons must always be a value added service to the guest. Then at the very least we should be able to exchange business cards with our clients. We just have to ask with confidence. Also try the method of turning the page to the guest to fill out. They will write it quicker and easier than us. You will also gain assurance with your guest when you ask them which number or medium is their preferred method of contact. Be sure to let them know their information is kept confidential. DO NOT use this info to put them on an e-mail or junk mail marketing list.

Once the information is obtained another hurdle you might face is again the fear of calling them. 'We don't want to be perceived as pushy.' As a manager I once received a request from a client to have my sales associate call him less. No problem, I let my associate know and the problem was solved. This guest bought about four to five times a year and always asked for his sales associate. This was the only time in 25 years I received such a request. Again most associates don't follow-up enough, even the best of us.

Set time aside for clienteling. Assign time to your associates when they don't have any other responsibilities, including waiting for or helping the next walk-in guest. It might be an hour or two a day. If a system is kept up this should be plenty, and the time spent will be productive. Further discussion on clienteling frequency and techniques will be covered in a later lesson.

You should host one-on-one meetings with your associates weekly. Have them bring to your desk, or private space, their client book, and show you what they are working on this week, what they did last week, and their plans for next week. They should show you client pages filled out completely with good follow-up notes. Share success stories and discuss opportunities for improvement. Continue to work with them daily with these plans on the sales floor.

MONTHLY EVENTS

Month _____

DATE	GUEST	EVENT	NOTES

SPECIAL ORDER/SERVICE DELIVERY LOG

Due Date	Client Name	Service/Product	Follow-Up

SALES PLANNER, YEAR

ASSOCIATE _____ YEAR _____

	LY $ Sold	TY $ Goal	TY $ Actual	$ +/-	% +/-
JAN					
TOTAL					
FEB					
TOTAL					
MARCH					
TOTAL					
APRIL					
TOTAL					
MAY					
TOTAL					
JUNE					
TOTAL					
JULY					
TOTAL					
AUG					
TOTAL					
SEPT					
TOTAL					
OCT					
TOTAL					
NOV					
TOTAL					
DEC					
TOTAL					

Ly = Last Year, TY = This Year

SALES PLANNER, MONTH

ASSOCIATE _____ MONTH _____

LY Actual _____ TY Goal _____ TY Stretch _____
Per Day _____ Per Day _____ Per Day _____

Day	Goal Accrue	Act. Daily	Act. Accrue	Accrue +/-
1				
2				
3				
4				
5				
6				
7				
8				
9				
10				
11				
12				
13				
14				
15				
16				
17				
18				
19				
20				
21				
22				
23				
24				
25				
26				
27				
28				
29				
30				
31				

Per Day = Average needed for Month Total, Act = Actual $ Sold

"I don't want to do business with those who don't make a profit, because they can't give the best service."

— Richard Bach

A LUXURY E-MAIL EXPERIENCE

E-mail has opened up new opportunities in the way of communication to and from our clients. While some clients would rather not have us call them, or are too busy to call us, e-mail can be discreet, secure, and efficient. E-mail can reach a client without disturbing them and lets them answer it at their convenience. We can use e-mail at any time of day, to make use of our down times. E-mail provides instant delivery and reply, and without paying for postage. Plus it offers opportunity to include photos or other attachments. And with some followed rules it can be a highly effective sales tool for us and a **Luxury Experience** for our clients.

Etiquette Rules

Rule #1, do not force your clients into providing their e-mail address. Always ask permission, or inform them that you will e-mail them. So many retailers are asking for e-mail addresses to add to their marketing databases. For our purpose in professional sales, we would want to inform our guests that we will not put them on a group marketing list and that their e-mail address will be kept private. If you don't explain this at the time of collecting the address you stand a good chance of getting the "junk box" e-mail address.

I, like many, keep three e-mail addresses; one for business, one for family and friends, then one to use for online purchases, retailers and solicitors. The third mentioned mail box is always full of unwanted junk no matter how much time I spend trying to "opt out". When I don't feel comfortable with the intended use of my address I give out the junk address. We do not want to be included in this box.

You should be able to tell from the address if it is their business e-mail with the @... informing you of their business name. This might be the preferred box for us as it will be check more often and have less junk going to it. Many use a portable e-mail device, (iPhone, Treo, Blackberry, etc.) making it even easier to reach them if you have the right address.

Rule #2, do not replace all phone calls with e-mail. A phone call is still more personable and can provide better two way conversations. E-mail needs to be limited to simple, clear communication. If you know more questions will come from your communication, call the client. Plus no matter how well written, an e-mail can not provide the pleasant tone of voice we can produce over the phone.

Human communication relies on body language, tone of voice, and words, in that order. When talking over the phone, tone of voice is still a stronger element than words. When we e-mail we are left with only words and a good chance of miscommunication or misunderstanding.

Try this exercise with your coworkers. Take turns saying the single word 'nice' to each other while changing your tone of voice each time. You will also give off body language without thinking about it. Now note how many meanings of this word gets expressed and perceived. In an e-mail without tone of voice or body language the attended meaning is up for grabs. When in doubt of a clear and concise message, please call your client.

Rule #3, use an informative subject line. Considering many clients will receive 40 to 200 e-mails in a single day, you want yours to clearly stand out.

I just opened my box to 96 e-mails. Step one was to checkmark the unwanted e-mails then click on the trashcan. I took a whopping 30 seconds to glance at the headings and trash all but 7 without opening them.

You must be informative but concise. Name the product, reason for purchase and client's name if applicable. IE; Diamond ring for Sara's birthday.

Also, spam filters could send your message to the junk box if you use some words like 'sale', 'free', 'special promotion', or the use of punctuation as simple as '!' or '$'. Visit Microsoft at http://office.microsoft.com/en-us/help/HA010450051033.aspx for a list of key words their programming uses to filter unwanted e-mails.

I once had a guest e-mail me a request for money back. I never received her e-mail because 'money back' was a key phrase sending her request to my junk box. You can imagine an already frustrated client wondering why I did not respond.

It is a good idea to check your junk box often and keep it cleaned out. Like a pile of mail, one might be the tax refund check. We must do everything possible to see that our guests receive the sought after communications. When in doubt, follow up your e-mail with a phone call.

Rule #4, write professionally. Do not use text message slang like UR, LOL, ☺, or IDK. I had to ask my teenager what some of this meant in text messages she was sending me. You have a full keyboard and spell check, use it.

Please do use a greeting and an ending as you would in any professional letter. IE; "Dear…, and Kind regards". (Don't use impersonal "dear friend" as this is on the spam filter list and you should have and use their name anyway.)

Include phone, e-mail, and mail contact information after your name. Many e-mail programs offer automatic signature lines that can be utilized for this purpose.

Use a professional, plain letter format. Avoid color or photo backgrounds or fancy script.

Keep the use of punctuations correct and professional. Do not use all CAPS as this sets the tone of raising your voice. HAVE I MADE MYSELF CLEAR!!!??

Rule #5, be clear and concise in your message. You must keep the body of your e-mail under a screen full or it will not be read completely, if at all. Remember our clients will have 40 or more waiting to be read so don't ramble.

Use one and two sentence paragraphs or bullet points to make it an easy format to read and understand. Assume your e-mail will be quickly scanned for the pertinent information so make it easy to find with very little clutter.

I read most of my e-mail off a Treo device and just received one today that rambled on for a page and a half. My Treo took twelve pages to display this letter. It was a request for help sent through a volunteer program I am part of. In the end I did not believe the story and opted out on this project. We as sales people are viewed as "fast talkers with an answer for everything." When we are too wordy we live up to this stereotype and no one has the time to read or listen.

Rule #6, proofread your e-mail. After using a spell check, re-read for correct grammar and essence. You could have done the spell check but still have a sentence like this. *"I had reduced to dollars of you're bananas."* when you meant to say *"I have reduced two dollars off your bananas."* Both go through the spell check just fine, but you could imagine the difference in client reaction to the two e-mails. Have someone else proofread to make sure the message is clear.

Double check the "To" box, making sure you are sending the e-mail to the right person. If you want to send a copy to include another associate, consider the Bcc function, (Blind carbon copy) in-order to keep this inclusion confidential. Make sure you have included any needed attachments and have made mention of these attachments in the body of the e-mail.

E-mail is a great time saver, but because of that we will get in the habit of rushing the process. Slow down and do it write, (I mean right, LOL) before hitting "SEND."

Rule #7, don't send an angry or negative tone e-mail. There is no way that mere words can properly express emotion as well as voice or body language. I am not saying to pick up a phone screaming or go to their house and make a scene. But an e-mail can be taken the wrong way and usually perceived more negative than attended. So when you even attempt to be a little sarcastic, it will be perceived much worse.

If you receive an angry e-mail, I find it best to call the guest instead of replying with another e-mail. A prompt call with a caring voice will change the tone and smooth things over. If you have no phone number then you might reply with your willingness to help and the best phone number you can be reached to discuss further.

Never let "Reply" chats go back and forth more than a couple of times. This is a clear sign that a phone call or face to face meeting is needed. If you feel the need to send anything in the least bit negative, sleep on it overnight. You will handle the communication in a more positive manner the next day.

Also keep in mind; an e-mail creates a written document, a document that can be printed, forwarded, cut and pasted and even blogged on the internet. Don't ever write something that you would not want published for others to see.

Rule #8, be timely on e-mails sent and replies back. We as retail salespeople have many duties to perform, a large sales floor to cover and long hours to work. But when we use e-mail as communication a problem with promptness can arise. Many clients assume we will receive their e-mail instantly as if we are sitting at a desk with the popup screen flashing in front of us.

Please check your incoming e-mails and junk box several times a day if possible. Then respond immediately if at all possible. If you don't have the information they ask for at your finger tips, respond immediately with a quick note that you are working on it and when you will get back to them.

Another thing to consider is an auto reply message to all incoming e-mails if you cannot check your box often. Most e-mail programs have this feature and can inform your client you are away from your desk but will return their e-mail within a few hours. This is at least better than not knowing if the e-mail was received or when the response will be returned.

Rule #9, go the extra mile with service. E-mail and the internet can be wonderful tools for sales success. A clear informative e-mail can be very welcomed. Plus if you can include something extra to help your client make the needed decision to buy or clear up any confusion then you will find even more success using this communication method.

They say a photo is worth a thousand words, so attach a good clear photo of the product you are discussing on your e-mail. Including this whether requested or not will greatly enhance the experience and help bring the focus back to the product and why we are communicating in the first place. If you do not have a photo inventory of your products, use the internet to search, save, and attach one to your e-mail. Don't go wild; just the top one or two choices should be enough.

Another function that can be useful if used carefully is links to yours or another website for more information. Providing enough information to make the buying decision is our job. The internet can provide that when we find the right websites. But too many or the wrong sites can produce confusion or information overload. Or if we over educate, than we are no longer needed and the client can buy off of the internet or a discount warehouse. We just worked for free. So again, be careful.

A luxury shopping experience is one that comfortably and graciously guides us thru the investigate, purchase, and consume process, without the need or desire to look elsewhere. We can provide this experience with careful use of all our resources including e-mail.

Key Points

- Obtain the best address and ask permission to use it.
- Assure your guest you will not place them on a mailing list and that you will keep their address confidential.
- Remember e-mail does not always replace a friendly phone call.
- Make sure your e-mail gets past the spam filters and your subject line creates interest to open.
- Write professionally.
- Keep the text body clear, concise and less than a page long.
- Proofread. You can not change a thing once you click send.
- Double check that you are sending the e-mail to the right person. This is a very common mistake. Also check that the desired attachments are included.
- Watch the tone of your e-mail.
- Do not e-mail anything you would not want forwarded or publicly transmitted.
- Be timely with your e-mails and replies. Check your box often.
- Add an extra service like a product photo or helpful link.

Manager's Notes

If your staffing is like mine, you will have many levels of experience with e-mail and the internet within your staff. Use the more experienced to help train the less experienced. Also use the better English writers in your staff to help proofread others.

I recommend that you have your staff Bcc you on all e-mails. This will give you a chance to monitor and provide feedback to your associates and keep your finger on the pulse of the business. Some computer servers might be able to automatically send you a copy of all e-mails leaving your office. Ask your IT manager.

Also use e-mail to communicate between staff members when they are off for the day. This will create a record of messages; phone calls missed, client visits and even store memos that they can't miss. Plus it is yet another great reason for them to check their mail box more often.

On the next page I have a sample e-mail to a client after a store shopping visit. You could make several samples for your particular business. Again, delegate this task to some of the more experienced and watch them rise to the challenge.

Sample E-Mail

To: johndoe@anymail.com
Cc: _____
Bcc: mymgr@bruce'sstore.net

Subject: Ring details for Amy's birthday
Attachment: img-Amy'snewring

Dear John,
It was a pleasure meeting you today at Bruce's Store.

I have the details below as promised for Amy's ring;
- Diamond quality as we discussed
- Center diamond wt; 1.50ct, total side diamond wt; 1.00ct.
- Ring made from platinum
- Finger size 5.5
- Delivery promise date; March 3rd if ordered this week
- Your final price; $31,500
- Half down will get the order started

Attached is a photo of the completed ring.

You may visit our informative website; www.bruce'sstore.net to explain more about your purchase, and call me at the number below. We can handle the transaction over the phone.

I appreciate the opportunity to help you and look forward to hearing the story of when you present this fabulous ring to Amy.

Kind regards,
Bruce

Bruce Eicher
AGS Certified Sales Associate
Bruce's Store
Luxury Shopping Mall
777-555-1234 bruceeicher@bruce'sstore.net

HARNESS THE POWER OF EMOTIONS

When you truly comprehend the shopping and buying process, you will discover it to be full of emotions. It does not matter if it is at a hardware store, clothing boutique, camera showcase, or a perfume counter; each purchase will be an emotional experience. If we can identify some of the key emotions our guests are (or should be) experiencing, we can harness these feelings and easily close and add-on to our sale.

Why People Shop and Buy

We all shop every week to fill needs. We will go to the grocery store with a list, say milk, eggs, bread, and butter. But we hardly ever leave with just those items. We might add popcorn so we can enjoy a movie. Or we might change from brown bread to French bread for French toast. What we have done is turned ordinary shopping into a little more, something to create an experience.

If I am buying nails at the hardware store it awakens emotion. You now think I'm crazy, but as I pick out my needed nails I am thinking about how satisfying the physical work of hammering will be. Not only will it remove stress but in the end I will be able to stand back and admire my work, created with my hands. Stress relief, pleasure and pride, and that's just nails; don't even get me started on tool shopping.

Life Moments

So it is not just stuff in a shopping basket. They are products that will help provide **Life Moments** or memories. **Life Moments** are high points in time that the experience and emotions felt overcome anything we had to do to get there. Like The Game of Life with Life cards, we advance many spaces when we enjoy these moments. And we need help to discover and put these **Life Moments** together. A good salesperson can be of assistance.

The Two Types of Needs

There are two types of needs people fulfill when they shop, **Functional Needs and Emotional Needs**. We should always ask our guests, "Why are you shopping today?" It is an excellent open-ended question that demands a response we can use to assist them better. But we must understand; the answer we get back will be the **Functional Need** in most cases. For example; a man saying he is shopping for his wife's anniversary is a functional reason. (Yes I know I said "his wife's anniversary". This is a very common expression, one that I will let psychologists decipher.) But the **Emotional Need** you can harness is the man's need to provide, or his desire to demonstrate his success. And it should also be a need to show his wife how much he loves and appreciates her. <u>These are the **core shopping and buying reasons**. The anniversary is just his excuse and provides urgency for the purchase.</u>

Clerked Transaction

We have all heard the expression, "it's the thought that counts." So with that in mind any small trinket would fulfill the functional need of the anniversary.

For instance; a customer asks to see anniversary rings. The associate shows the collection of rings and gives him the price range. The client assumes any will fill his anniversary gift needs and buys one of the least expensive. No personal questions were asked, no emotional buildup of the gift giving occasion was done. Nor was there any mention of how the ring represents his love for his wife. The customer buys but leaves only somewhat fulfilled.

Many times I have seen just that happen, even with a professional salesperson helping a client. That is called a **Clerked Transaction**. We filled only his **Functional Need**. But what if we wanted to fulfill the **Emotional Need**? You bet, we would have a much larger sale, because the client is filling the core reason he was shopping, not just the excuse.

It will take some additional conversation to uncover many of the core buying emotions. Like with the gentleman shopping for his wife's anniversary, you might follow-up with the questions; "How many years have you been married?" and "She is very special to you, isn't she?" So the conversation turns to his wife and the love he has for her. You are building up, romancing, and adding perceived value to the reason he is shopping. Now we can make some product suggestions to fill his core need, the expressing of his appreciation and immense love for his wife. And with the core need exposed you can show big, flatter and excite him. **Dazzle** him.

I'm Just Looking

"I'm Just Looking" will be a response we hear many times when we ask "Why are you shopping today?" This response is a defensive measure to maintain a wall or space between you and them. The guest may not be quite ready for your assistance, need some space, or have a fear of being pressured into buying. Another explanation is that the core reason they are shopping lays deeper than they wish to reveal or even understand themselves. They are shopping to fill an emotional void or need like jealousy, keeping up with the Joneses, depression, loneliness or simply entertainment.

After the just looking response I use a three step process I call **AWC; Affirm, Warm and Connect**. First; defuse the defenses with an acknowledgement **Affirming** their wishes. I like the phrase "Please take your time looking, but I am here to assist you when you need." Pause and let those words sink in. Then; **Warm** them by using perks and services you have developed in the "Oasis" and "Serve" chapters. Offer one or two of these to your guest, IE; drink, cleaning, or service checkup. Now give them a little space while you get the drink and pass the service to a teammate.

The last step is to **Connect** with your guest. Many a times I have successfully used the **Dazzle** process to connect with a stubborn guest. When I bring the **Dazzle** product to them (or them to it) I will use the phrase "here's something you have got to take a *look* at." This again affirms that they are "just looking." Remember, when done right the **Dazzle** process will flatter and excite them. Then they should be ready to open up and you can uncover their reasons for shopping.

Fill the Emotional Need

There can be nothing more powerful than emotion. When we learn to tap into the emotions of buying we open up an expressway to success. I have often heard, after a guest departs without purchasing, the sales associate say "we had just what he asked for, but he would not buy." What I have found in many of these cases is the sales associate attempted to fill only the **Functional Need** and failed to satisfy the **Emotional Need**.

All products, in some shape or form, fill a **Functional Need**. We have all learned how to ask our guests questions to determine their needs. And we will fit their needs with a product. We then present features and benefits on how our products fill the needs, and we try to close the sale.

So much of our training is focused on product knowledge; technical information on what our product is, will do, and perform. This is important knowledge to possess. Product knowledge gives us the confidence we need to sell, and our clients' confidence in us to buy. And we should also know how to take the product features and turn it into a benefit fitted to the client's needs.

What many sales associates don't know (or utilize) is that there are two types of benefits for each feature of your product. One benefit fills a **Functional Need** and the other fills an **Emotional Need**. For example; a fur on a coat keeps you warm but is also stylish and will make you feel good about how you look, a quality diamond in a ring shows you are married but is also able to make your friends green with envy, and a new camera's resolution will take great pics but also records your life events and gives high quality results suitable for framing, hanging and showing your house guests.

It is just a matter of <u>taking the benefits a step further, into the end use and results of your product in their life;</u> **Life Moments**. Keep the client's tastes, interests, and desires in-mind as you create their moments of use and enjoyment. What you want to do is hit his or her "hot button", the one or two things that will make the difference for them to buy.

The Gifting Moment

If you are selling a gift there will be additional **Life Moments** of emotion to build excitement in your product. This I call the **Gifting Moment**. Ask your client early in the product presentation how he or she plans on presenting the gift. Be ready with some creative ideas to help them create this special moment. Talk up the gifting moment, letting the client know how surprised and appreciative the receiver will be.

I often told my male engagement ring clients; "The first thing your fiancée's friends and sisters will do is grab her hand and take a close look at the ring, then they will ask, 'how did he propose?" Next, after offering a tissue to wipe his forehead, I reassure him that I will help him pick the perfect diamond ring, and then assist him on how to pop the question. No internet site or warehouse outlet will identify and fulfill these overlooked needs or help create these **Life Moments**.

Awaken the Analytical

As you know, there are two different ways to make any decision; analytical or emotional, left brain or right brain as many studies refer. If you have an emotional thinking client, your job can be easier. They are already thinking the way we want them, and we just need to identify and satisfy their **Emotional Need**. We won't have to get too technical, if at all. We just need to give them the features and benefits of our products related to the emotions they wish to satisfy.

Now when we have an analytical thinker, we must both satisfy their need for information and also awaken the emotional side in them. The payoff with this type of client can be huge. Awakening emotions and filling a void that has been missing can be a powerful experience, one that will create a strong desire for more. You will create a loyal client, always asking for you. You could be their "you complete me" from a 90's movie.

Analytical shoppers are often shopping with the intent to gather information. Your job is to satisfy enough of their informational hunger to make them comfortable and to build confidence in you as their advisor. Don't oversell on product knowledge alone, lest you educate them a sufficient amount to buy at a discount warehouse or on-line. Once you have their confidence in you as their advisor then you can interpose the emotional side of the shopping experience.

There will be many times when you will have to lead the client into emotional thoughts. Precede through your selling process, interjecting emotional reasons why to buy, give, and own your products. Talk about the **Life Moments** the product will bring, IE; a romantic drive to the beach in their new car, the wearing of a new suit at a business meeting, or showing your friends and sisters your new diamond ring.

Do not assume they will connect the dots between the product features, **Functional Benefits** and **Emotional Benefits**. Likewise, they will not imagine the **Gifting Moment** and **End Use Life Moments** they can experience with the help of your products. You must connect the dots, and then paint the picture for them. Make it full color.

Key Points

- There are two types of needs filled with shopping and buying; **Functional Needs** and **Emotional Needs**.
- The **Emotional Needs** are the **Core** shopping and buying reasons. Exposing the **Core Need** will put a greater importance and worth on the shopping occasion.
- Use **A**ffirm, **W**arm, and **C**onnect with "just lookers."
- Filling just the **Functional Needs** leads to a minimal, **Clerked Transaction**.
- Building up and selling to the **Core Need** will produce a bigger ticket and have a greater improved chance of closure.
- Analytical thinkers need their emotional side awakened.
- Avoid selling for the competition by over-educating.
- Do not assume your guest will connect the dots to the **Emotional Benefits** or build their own **Life Experience** images. Paint the whole picture.
- **Steps to Harnessing the power of emotions:**

    o Ask your guests; "Why are you shopping today?" to uncover the **Functional Need**, the justification.
    o Ask follow-up questions to turn the functional excuse into the **Emotional Core Need**.
    o Identify the emotions your clients are, or should be feeling.
    o Build and romance the **Core** reasons your client is shopping to add perceived value.

- o Show big, flatter and excite your guest, **Dazzle**.
- o Use features and benefit statements, with both **Functional** and **Emotional Benefits**.
- o Satisfy informational, technical information as needed to gain your clients confidence. Be their advisor, and then add the emotional side of the shopping experience.
- o Paint a picture for your client of **Gifting Moments** and **Life Moments** with your products, keeping them aligned with your client's desires.

Why are you shopping today? = Functional Need + Follow-Up Questions = Emotional, Core Need.

Product Feature + Functional Benefit + Emotional Benefit + Life Moments = Larger, easier sales.

Manager's Notes

In-order to apply this lesson to your particularly business I have an exercise for you to do. With your team, list all the answers you would get to the question; "Why are you shopping today?" Then take the answers and convert them to what **Emotional Needs** you would be satisfying. Continue to list other emotional reasons people shop, like entertainment, jealousy, keeping up with the Joneses, depression, or loneliness.

From your lists indentify the emotional shopping reasons that might produce the "I'm just looking" phrase.

Add to the list follow-up questions that can be used for each functional shopping reason that will help uncover the core, emotional reason. Questions or phrases that will bring out the emotional thoughts your clients are, or should be feeling when shopping and buying.

Finally, make a list of your products. Add to each product both the **Functional** and the **Emotional Benefits** it can offer. Then write the **Gifting Moments** and **End-Use Moments** they will provide.

These **Life Moments** take place in the future, way **Past Your Cash Register**.

*Long after the money spent is forgotten, the product will be providing or assisting in these **Life Moments**.*

Print and post these lists so they can be read many times. We should become comfortable in using these with role-plays and live practice.

Practice the "I'm just looking" response process; **A**ffirm, **W**arm, and **C**onnect till smooth.

Draw yourself a LIFE card.

"It is reckless to pay too much, but it is worse to pay too little. When you pay too much it's true you may loose a little money, but that is where it ends.
When you pay too little you risk everything because what you have purchased is not able to do the job you purchased it for. Common business law makes it impossible to pay little and get lots: this cannot happen.
If you deal with the lowest offer you should remember to build up a certain reserve fund to cover the risk you are taking.
But if you can do this then you certainly also have enough money to buy something better."

— John Ruskin

BUILDING VALUE ABOVE THE PRICE

With The New Retail Climate consumers are buying fewer items. They are shopping less. And they want more for their money. But that's OK. More for their money translates to longer life, non-disposable, less trendy, more classic, and better quality. And these are qualities with that we can build value and harness emotions. But first let's talk about price.

The Anxiety of Price

Price is always a fantastic source of anxiety, anxiety for both the salesperson and the client. Most customers are afraid to ask the price, or if there is a discount available. They wonder what hidden costs or add-ons will be needed. And they are unsure that they are shopping in the right store for the best deal. These concerns are amplified when anyone is shopping for luxury goods.

On the flip side, sales associates can be fearful that they are charging too much for their products and services. Salespeople will often pre-judge a client based on age, dress or other appearances and present less expensive products. (Or worse yet, assume they are not capable of buying and give up selling them altogether.)

Also many associates sell using their pocketbook as the scale of worth. So many times we will be helping clients with much larger incomes than ours, yet we still assume they will want lower priced products, ones that we could afford. What might be perceived as expensive or overpriced to you will seem fair or even underpriced to others. <u>Nothing is overpriced unless you can find the exact same product, readily available, with the same services, for less.</u>

Our Confidence Is Paramount

In-order to provide a luxury experience and to close the sale we need to create confidence with our prices. The confidence has to start with you, the salesperson.

The first step is to study your products. What all do they do, how are they made, where are they made, and how do they perform? And compare them to their competitors' in performance, quality, appearance, and price.

Then you need to take a good look at your company. What perks and services do you offer compared to your competition? Since you are the one reading this book, I bet you are ahead of most, if not all of them. Remember, just the experience your guests have in your store will greatly add to the value of your products.

Now, with the above information gathered, shop several of your closest competitors. Investigate their products, pricing and what services they offer. Take a notice of the stores atmosphere and quality of their salespeople. You should come back with a list of their strengths and weaknesses compared to yours. Use this list to further the value you offer.

In the end result you should have a longer list of why to buy your products and do business with you and your company, then why to buy at the competition. And this should give you the confidence needed for the rest of this lesson.

Price Is a Functional Need

The price or dollar amount of a product is nothing but numbers. It is not a measure of performance or quality. It will not determine what the product will cost per day of use or enjoyment. It will not reflect the actual outcome of your client's satisfaction. It does not tell the whole story of cost; <u>price reveals only what digits will be printed on the credit card slip, today.</u>

Whether your products are clearly marked or not at all, early in your presentation price will come up. Your guest may not have any idea what to expect in the way of price. But they will have some idea of what your product, at this time, is worth to them. I say "at this time" because we have not yet built the value of our product.

With you presentation, I hope you have correctly started with your highest end product. Remember the **Dazzle** technique; start with you most expensive, flatter and excite them with your best. When the guest asks for the price, your answer of the dollar amount fills the **Functional Need**. We must express this dollar amount with a clear and confident voice while maintaining eye contact. Watch their body language and be ready for a response. With showing your most expensive, you have forced the uncomfortable subject of price to surface, and you have nowhere to go but towards more comfortable. Depending on their reaction, you can lessen their anxiety with either building value in the top shelf product, or by giving them a less expensive alternative. Either way, you have the subject of price on the table and are willing and able to make it more comfortable.

Within your product presentation, price should be a short conversation. You might have to explain discounts if offered, or reassure your client why you are a non-discount store. Then the conversation could turn to alternate methods of payments, such as in-store financing. Price only needs to be addressed to the point of making sure you are within the client's means, that he or she can afford it if they choose.

Value Is an Emotional Need

Like other **Emotional Needs**, value is the **Core Need** and is hidden behind its **Functional Need**, price. Value is tied directly to the emotion of confidence. Your client needs to feel confident that they are not spending too much for a product that does too little.

It would be safe to assume that everyone needs some value emotion satisfied before they make a buying decision. This is especially true if they are spending more than they expected before coming into your store. Be their advisor; ask questions to get their **Core Needs** understood. Then address those **Core Needs** with **Value Statements** and **End-Use Stories** that will raise their perceived value in your products.

I was shopping for a computer to give my teenage daughter at Christmas. I pre-shopped online before driving to my local computer store. They had a couple of laptops advertised on sale and the website showed them in stock at the local store. I still wanted to talk to someone and get their educated opinion. In the store I asked the salesperson about the advertised items and for his recommendation. He asked me questions that led to the **End-Use** of the laptop. Long story short, I left with a more advanced model at a higher price than I had planned. But I was very pleased to find for a little more money, I was able to present my daughter with a computer that she could also use for college in two years. I feel I received more for my money than if I would have spent less on a computer lasting only for a year or two.

In the above example, the questions that opened up the **Core Value Needs** were; "Who's the computer for?" "How old is she?" and "Does she plan on going to college?" He also asked, "Would I like to buy one computer for now plus a new one for college, or would I rather spend a little extra at this time and have it last through her education?" I replied, "yes, I would rather do it all with one." And in the product presentation, the salesman stated, "This higher end model will not only last her for many years but also give her smoother, more reliable performance through college graduation." This last statement put my mind way past the moment of spending the money and into the **Life Moments** of my girl going to college and graduating. It is what I call a **Value Statement**, a statement that pointed out both an increase in time and quality of product service I would receive. And it was tailored to fit my **Core Needs**.

Past the Register

The **Value Statement** also made my mind fast forward with daydream thoughts of the future. Your product **Value Statements** and **End-Use Stories** can, and should have this effect on your clients. This is what I have called **putting them past the register**. They are no longer thinking or worrying about spending the money; they are mentally owning the goods and having **Life Moments** with them.

It was a simple and logical outcome to buy the more expensive computer. But it took a salesperson's help to get me to that point of emotional satisfaction in the product we chose.

Selling Luxury Goods

In the luxury product business there is a unique phenomenon. With an outrageously high priced product, the price itself can be the feature and allure. A name brand product, priced above logical reason and out of reach of the average consumer will attract attention and create demand. You could look at several handbag, clothing, jewelry, timepiece and auto companies to see examples of this occurrence. Or you can see this in many branded companies, store names that have built a reputation of high prices and quality or service. Just to buy, own, or gift something from one of these stores has a strong appeal. While the quality of the product might only be slightly above average the price can be two to ten times the average price. With these products the emotional desire filled is exclusivtivity, status, and vanity. As a salesperson you need to play up this exclusive product with statements on how it will show off your clients' success or set them apart from their peers.

While selling luxury goods, many guests will not be able to understand the price. With most luxury products you can not defend the higher price with just factual statistics or performance numbers. Some brands can just cost more even though their performance is the same. But that does not mean they don't have added value. The value might just be in peace of mind that you have bought the best, most respected brand. So we are back to an emotion, peace of mind. Many other emotions can be satisfied with luxury goods. I will leave it up to you to develop this list of emotional values for your products. Please take pride in your high prices.

We All Need a Story

Every product brand, category or even model in your store needs a story. The story is one you tell a prospective buyer that might entice them to own that particular product. It is a story they can retell their friends and family when they showoff their new purchase. I call it the **Designer Story**.

Though the name implies that the products needs to be from a fashion designer, this is not so. Any product can have a story about what makes it better, unique and desirable.

Let me give you an example of a watch's designer story. *The designer, Frank Gourald received his inspiration for the shape of this timepiece from the historic F-35 stealth jet. The case is made from the same metal alloy as the jet and the hands are in the shape of the defense missiles it carried. All production from start to finish is done by hand in Switzerland and takes over 150 man hours to produce each watch. This same timepiece is worn by the pilots who fly the F-35. Plus it's built in emergency locating transmitter and GPS has been credited in saving twenty-seven lives in the last five years. Frank Gourald also designed the timepieces to be given to each passenger on the first private flights to orbit the moon. This particular watch is number 35 of 100 in a limited edition series.* If this watch existed I would buy it after hearing this story, and then tell all my friends parts of the story.

While your products might not orbit the moon, they should have some designer story. In high-end fashion you should know something about the designer. Where they grew up, where they live. What are their design inspirations? What else have they designed and for who. In all products you need to know where the products are produced. What are some of the manufacturing processes or materials that make them unique? Just a few quick statements for each brand or label are needed.

Then I believe the most powerful story segment can be who wears, uses, or drives your products. Ask your manufactures for information. Many might keep records and photos of famous people with their products. Read your industry magazines and always search fashion and people magazines for candid product use shots. You could even start a scrapbook to show your store guests. My wife wears some jewelry designs that have also been worn and photographed on famous music artists. You can bet this adds value for her and gives a story she can tell when someone compliments her taste. It is a strong endorsement of the products quality and fashion statement when a public figure uses your product. The famous person can as well be your manager, another sales associate, family, or a good friend. It would provide comfort to know these people selected this product too.

Last but not least, collect success stories where the product has been put into use successfully. These stories should exhibit how your product made for a **Life Experience**, if at all possible. They would most likely come from stories you heard from other clients, or it could be from personal experience. (Don't use your clients' names, or you risk breaking confidentiality.) Some products, like deluxe electric can openers, won't directly create life experiences. But they might make a task easier and quicker, then allowing more free time for the family picnic.

In the end, <u>we must present the core value benefits, which fit the client's needs, outweighing the amount of money needed to purchase the product.</u> In fact, <u>the client should purchase, not even thinking about the money spent, but looking forward to the pleasure that the product will bring.</u>

Key Points

- Both the customers and the sales associates can fear talking about price.
- The fear or anxiety over price increases for luxury goods.
- Many associates incorrectly use their pocketbook as the scale of worth, and undersell their clients.
- Nothing is overpriced unless you can find the exact same product, readily available, with the same services, for less.
- Price reveals only what digits will be printed on the credit card slip today.

- The price is a **Functional Need**.
- The conversation of price should be short, revealing whether the chosen product is within the client's means.
- Value, tied to confidence is the **Core Need** hidden behind price.
- Uncover, and then attend to **Core Needs** with **Value Statements** and **End-Use Stories**.
- In luxury goods the high price is the feature and allure.
- You can not defend luxury prices with product specifications. You must appease emotions.
- Many products have a story to tell, please write them and tell them.
- Use these **Designer Stories** to create **Life Moments** fitted to your client.
- **Core Value Benefits**, which fit the client's **Emotional Needs,** must outweigh the amount of money needed to purchase the product.

Manager's Notes

Like the previous chapter I have assignments to help apply this lesson to your business.

First, shop your competition. Delegate this task out so you can visit them all. Shop them for like products, price, and services. Make note of their strengths and weaknesses. Compare these notes with your company. Use these comparisons to better your store and to build confidence in your prices and values offered.

Next, working together write these lists and stories;
- List emotions you should appease with your products.
- Write **Value Statements** to address your product cost and appease the emotions.
- Write product brand, **Designer Stories** that will entice the consumer to own them.
- Write **End-Use Success Stories** to further confidence in the product value.

Practice talking about price, and then turning the conversation to **Value Statements** and **Emotion Benefits** fitted for your clients. Practice the **Designer Stories** and **End-Use Success Stories** till smooth and alluring.

A luxury shopping experience is one that comfortably and graciously guides us thru the investigate, purchase, and consume process, without the need or desire to look elsewhere.

CLOSE ON THE EMOTIONAL HIGH

With the last two lessons we have learned to harness the power of emotions to create both a stronger desire and a greater worth of our products. Now we have the simple task of closing the sale.

Many selling statistics correctly state that a large percentage of sales are lost because the associate failed to ask for the sale. What I am going to tell you is; <u>don't ask for the sale, assume and take the sale!</u> If you have done as I have outlined leading up to this point, the client has all but forgotten the small transaction exchange of money detail. You just need to take care of it, <u>now!</u>

The **Core Emotional** reasons for shopping have been exposed. The emotions have been built-up and enhanced. With our **End-Use** and **Designer Stories** the client is in a dream-like state, using, gifting, and showing off the new purchase. With this process you have put your guest way **Past the Cash Register** and into the **Life Moments**. The desire for the product is at its peak. Their heart is racing. Before the adrenaline runs out, it is time to wrap up the sale and make the transaction. Take their money!

Watch the Signs

I get this heart racing excitement when I buy, especially if it is an expensive, out of budget impulsive purchase. While it is not quite like jumping out of an airplane, it is a thrill to buy. This excitement will produce body language that we can see.

As you create **Life Moments** for your clients, watch their body language. If they are holding, touching, wearing, or sitting in the product, that is a positive sign. If they are looking deeply through the product, they are daydreaming owning the product. Even a shaky hand or a bead of sweat on their brow is a positive sign, just a little nervous plus excited. In a nut shell, are they showing signs of being **Past the Register**?

Let's take a further look at my computer purchase for an example. Recall the associate built value and desire using **Life Moments**. *"This higher end model will not only last her for many years but also give her smoother, more reliable performance through college graduation."* I was fingering the keyboard and looking into the screen as he made this **Value Statement**. Then as I folded the computer he stated *"I will get you one in a box, and then I'll show you some bags to protect it when she travels."*

The salesman saw I was daydreaming about my girl using the computer at college. And the folding of the unit signified I was mentally taking it with me.

Use an Assumption Close

An **Assumption Close** does not ask for the sale, it assumes the sale and smoothly takes care of the transaction. <u>If we were to ask for the sale, it would require the client to come out of his daydream and mentally come to the cash register to think about and answer your question. This would spoil their **Life Moment** and our work to get them there.</u>

In our example he then stated, *"I will get you one in a box, then I'll show you some bags to protect it when she travels."* He assumed the sale with the "I will get one in a box" statement, he did not ask for my permission. Now, think about the added phrase, "…then I'll show you some bags to protect it when she travels." This **Assumption Close** with the added phrase still gives me a choice, whether or not to buy a bag. I like this added choice as a consumer; it makes me feel I am still making my own choices. Plus it sets up the transaction for an add-on sale.

Another example of an **Assumption Close** can be simply getting out a client card and asking for the information as the client would like it on the sales slip. If it is a gift you could ask "Should we put the warranty in your daughter's name?" This is your close; you just quickly and smoothly went on with completing the transaction.

Keep Them in the Life Moment

Again, we do not want to spoil the moment and drag their mind to the money being spent. The **Assumption Close** should be worded in a way to keep them in the **Life Moment**. For example; if you have your client in the **Gifting Moment**, use the closing question "I'll wrap it in gold foil, would she like a red or silver ribbon?" This paints a picture of the wrapped package in his **Gifting Moment**. And it gives him a choice of ribbon color, but assumes his choice to buy.

And we are not done looking at the computer close. The simple "…when she travels" phrase keeps me **Past the Cash Register** and in the **Life Moment** of my girl growing up and traveling to college.

Once we have the positive nod, it is imperative we make the transaction smooth and quick. Many times a simple credit card swipe is all we need, just ask "Do you have a card you wish to use?" Or we need to team up with our cashier to take care of the transaction while we go over product details or talk about end-use. If it is for a gift talk to them about the **Gifting Moment**, and give them ideas on how to make it extra special. You should not leave your client. If you do you will risk loosing the sale as they might snap out of the **Life Moment** and bolt.

Nothing to Loose

You have nothing to loose when you assume and take the sale. The worse that could happen is the client would say something like "Wait a minute, I have not yet decided." You then would follow up with something like "No hurry, let me show you a feature I would have loved on my computer when I was in college." So you are back to creating more **Life Moments** using product features with **Emotional Benefits**.

Also with a rejection of your closing you will get direction. The client may say no to buying, but human nature will force them to give you some reason. Many times this new information would not surface had it not been for the attempted close. With this information you can acknowledge and overcome their objective or pick a better suited product. You did not loose a thing and you gained new information and direction.

Key Points

- You have them at the peek of desire, now is the time to complete the transaction.
- You have the client **Past the Cash Register** and into **Life Moments.**
- Watch body language for ownership signs.
- Don't *ask* for the sale, assume and take the sale.
- *Asking* for the sale would spoil the **Life Moments** and mentally drag them to the register to choose.
- Use an **Assumption Close**.
- Give the **Assumption Close** a small choice for the client.
- Add a phrase to your close that will keep the client in their **Life Moment**.
- Make the money transaction smooth and quick.
- Do not leave your client or your risk losing the sale.
- You have nothing to loose and everything to gain with assuming and taking the sale.
- Even rejection comes with new information and direction.

Manager's Notes

Make a list of emotions that we experience at the time of making a buying decision. Emotions like "heart racing excitement" when we make an impulsive purchase out of our budget should be on top of your list. These are the emotions our guests should be feeling. We as salespeople need to mirror these feelings, taking our guests with us for the ride. Add to each emotion the body language we would likely observe from our guests.

Next develop a list of your teams favorite **Assumption Closes**. Word each to assume the close but add a further choice like the color of ribbon or an add-on item for the client to choose. Then to the list of closes add a phrase as needed to keep the client in the **Life Moment**.

Post these lists in your break room.

Practice identifying body language associated with the ownership and buying emotions. Role-play using your closes and phrases keeping the client in the **Life Moment**.

One more thing; take a good look at your cash/sales counter procedures. Is the process organized and swift? Or is it like a fire drill in the middle of the night? Do we know what to do if a credit card is declined? If you have in-store credit, is it also as easy and fast as possible? Are associates teaming up well with the office staff, keeping with the client at all times? Does the cashier have all the information needed from the sales associate to ring the sale? I have seen too many times, sales lost at the counter because of each one of these reasons. Eliminate that possibility and make it quick and smooth.

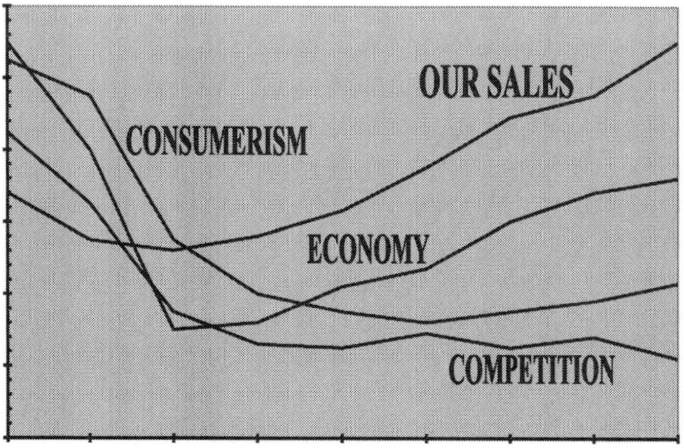
OUR SALES
CONSUMERISM
ECONOMY
COMPETITION

MORE CLIENTS, MORE OFTEN, SPENDING MORE MONEY

Clienteling is the act of personally marketing yourself and your business to previous and potential customers. That being said, many sales associates just scratch the surface with clienteling. But if we put some time and effort into this act, the reward can be huge.

Clienteling is not cold calling. It should not be a random process of card mailings. Nor is it huge e-mail blasts to your entire database. (Though group e-mails can be an effective, low cost means of selective advertising.) But clienteling is one-on-one sales associate to customer communications. Communications tailored for each client's needs and potentials.

What we need to establish is a working system to identify our clients that have the potential for growth and a process to grow and harvest their potential.

80% From 20%

The 80/20 rule came from the Pareto's Principle; 80 percent of the world's wealth is owned by 20 percent of its population. Then the same formula has been applied to business marketing; (and research generally finds it to hold true) 80 percent of your company's revenue is generated from 20 percent of your clients. Some might read this statistic and think, "Bingo! I only need to focus on that 20 percent." Many more believe that they are already serving that 20 percent just-fine-thank-you-very-much and turn all their efforts to developing new business. But the real value lies in understanding how to serve and cultivate our best clients. We cannot be everything to everybody. We need to concentrate our efforts on the highest probability of prospective. To that end, here are seven simple rules and steps for maximizing your clienteling potential.

Know Your Top 20 Percent

Many store's personnel might know who some of their top clients are, and you should. But with a little research you might find some surprising results you were unaware of. Please run reports from your computer sales database. These purchase history reports should be programmed to list the top clients by dollar amount spent. Use a total dollar amount that will list only the top 20 to 25 percent of your customer count. Go back five or more years.

Any names surprise you? I know I need to run this list a few times a year to stay current on my top clients. Some clients are in and out so quickly that we don't realize how much they are spending or how often. Many exceptional clients are low maintenance, but should they be taken for granted? No. We tend to remember the high maintenance customers, and this is not usually the best client, based on dollars spent.

Now take these top client lists and compare them to the sales associates' client books. First off, is there a principal sales associate assigned to each client? There should be and it should be only one associate or a team of two. Please see the "Team-Work" lesson for further information on principle associate assignment.

Now comb the client pages. Do we have one for each of the top 20 percent? Is the client's information complete and correct? IE: contact information, purchase history, personal interests, and life event dates. And does the associate have records of follow-up and service contacts? Plus is there a current wish list?

Remember these are your top 20 percent and we should have all this and more. If no associate has a complete client page on any one of these clients, assign an associate to start one and take over this orphan client's future business. I have needed to do this anytime there is a turnover of associates. Match the client to the associate that will do the best job meeting their core needs.

Know When, Where, and Why Your Top 20 Percent Spend Their Money

We are all creatures of habit. The purchase history reports will show patterns of habit with our top clients. Take a good look at these reports. How many times are they purchasing a year? Compare the purchase dates with their life event dates. Which life events are we missing? Do you have some top 20 that have not purchased in a year, if so, why? Frequency and date of purchase is one of four elements to analyze.

Second, how much are they spending on an average purchase? What is their low and what was their highest purchase? How many items are they purchasing at a time?

Third, what product brands and product categories are they buying? Is it from the same category or brand, or spread throughout the store?

Fourth, why are they buying, functional reasons and emotional core reasons? Self purchase or for a gift? And for whom?

One other piece of the puzzle is where else besides your company do they do business. If you are in the luxury product business, where else do they spend discretionary income? Do they love cars, horses, or airplanes? Do they gamble or travel? Are they remodeling their home or putting three kids through college? What's your silent competition with each client? Any information you gather on the interests and spending habits will give you an edge. It will all relate back to their **Core, Emotional Needs** of spending money. <u>Tie your product tighter to their **Core Needs** then the opposition ties theirs and you will win.</u>

Keep The 20 Percent Happy

Don't get complacent. Send them timely greeting cards. Send them a gift, thanking them for their loyalty. Follow-up with past purchases to make sure they are satisfied. Support a charity that is near and dear to their heart. Volunteer your time to their charitable cause. Patronize their place of business.

Even if they some of your top 20 have not been able to do business with you in a while you still need to keep them happy. When the tide turns for them, they will remember you.

Cultivate and Harvest Uncovered Opportunities

As you look at the good news; these 20 percent spend a lot of money with you. The better news is that there are holes in the patterns, more paths to take, and larger mountains to climb, all with these same clients.

First, fill the holes; what life events are we missing or don't know about? Don't forget events like new home purchase, push gift, empty nest, and new grandchildren. Then we have business related events; expansion, promotion, sale of or retirement from. I strongly recommend you read local and state business magazines and papers. Your client's events will be in these pages. Once we know all the life events, pick the ones you would most likely sell to and why. Who do we need to help provide a gift? Are there opportunities coming up? How's the wish list in the client book, up to date? Do we need to call them, write them, or e-mail them? Act now.

Second; what product brands and categories do they buy? What would compliment each product to complete a theme or collection? What is new or hot from their favorite brand or designer? What product lines or categories are they missing entirely? Have you explored custom or one-of-a-kind goods with this client?

Third; how much are they spending on each item? And how many items per purchase? Again, people are creatures of habit. And we will remain in our comfort zone until challenged. Maybe they have been spending $5,000 three times a year. We must challenge them out of their comfort zone of price. Show them at least $10,000 or more next time. Even better, use the **Dazzle** process, then come back to $10,000 as needed. And **Harness the Power of Emotions** in your selling process. There, you just raised their comfort zone to $10,000. Next time or two, try $20,000.

With all the new information we have on our top clients, plus the new lessons we have learned on harnessing emotions, ask yourself, "How can I better fulfill my clients core needs?"

Groom Tomorrow's 20 Percent

Back to the other 80 percent of your clients; don't completely ignore this group. While they may not be bringing in the big bucks, some of your most eager supporters can be found here. They usually know they are the bread but not the butter of your business, so they are even more appreciative of professional, personalized service.

For example, while you can't send a holiday gift to all of your clients, you can send a card. And since they will generally have less face time with you than your larger clients, make the most of it, giving them your undivided attention and really listening to their needs. That way, when they do have more business to bring in, they'll think of you first. And remember, these people have friends, which brings us to…

Ask For Referrals

A referral from a happy client is worth more than all the advertising, sponsorships, and PR combined. It is also one of the highest compliments from a client to you when you receive one.

It is perfectly appropriate to tell a client that you are always looking for quality clients and you find that the highest quality comes from current, valued clients. They'll be flattered that you asked them as a valued client.

I have often worked with a in store referral reward program. When a current client refers another, and they purchase I would give the referring client a $100 gift certificate. You could make that a mall gift card or dinner certificate if you would like.

When you give out your business cards give a couple extra and ask them to refer and friend, family member or neighbor.

Do you have highly social and affluent clients? Select one and throw them a private after hour's party at your store. Have them invite their choice of friends and neighbors. Cater a light meal and drinks. Have live music. Bring in something special in the way of merchandise or personal appearance of a designer. And offer to donate a percentage of the night's proceeds to their school or favorite charity.

Do Not Cater To the Exceptions

Speaking of quality clients, I'm sure you have some who aren't. Identify them (hint; take a look at high return and exchange ratios or deep discounts that offer no profit) and stop putting too much energy there. Keep them happy but don't go asking for non-profitable business.

Another use of the 80/20 principle is 80 percent of your time will be spent serving 20 percent of your clients. Make sure there is a return for your efforts. You cannot waste your resources trying to serve high maintenance, low return customers. You now know who your top 20 percent are, cater to them, not to the exceptions. See, now you just made more time to cultivate the rest.

Another Story

I was shopping at my local Harley store for a birthday gift. The owner of the shop did mutual business with me and my friend, so I asked for his help. I was just purchasing an article of clothing but the conversation turned to our friend and the new ride he wanted. I let it spill that my friend's wife told him he would have to sell half his gun collection and one of his other motorcycles before he could buy another. (The friend is a great example of rampage consumerism.)

A few days later my friend rode up on his new dream ride. I asked him where he got it and he told me from the local shop. He then told me he could not believe the service he got from the owner.

The owner found a gun collector to buy many of his guns, and then called my friend asking if he would be interested in selling some of his collection. This opened up the subject of my friends dream ride. And a deal was made to a trade the other bike to boot.

The conversations and transaction was handled in a professional manner that my friend did not know the bike shop owner was tipped off by me. My friend was impressed. And the shop owner showed what I call a **Killer Instinct**.

A **Killer Instinct** is when we find creative ways to serve the customer and close the sale. We don't give up with a couple of objections tossed our way. We find ways to clear away obstacles for our guests. Then we call them with great ideas or good news. Think about how you can creatively serve your clients and have a **Killer Instinct**.

Key Points

- Clienteling is one-on-one communications between a sales associate and their client tailored for the client's core needs and potentials.
- We need to concentrate our efforts on the highest probability of prospective, the 20 percent.
- Know Your Top 20 Percent
    - o We need to use our purchase history database to identify our top 20 percent based on dollars spent.
    - o Compare the database list to associates client pages.
    - o Gather missing information, assign orphan clients and build wish lists.
- Know The Top 20 Percent's Spending Patterns
    - o Our clients are creatures of habit.
    - o Know each clients average, high and low spending history. Then stretch their comfort zone.
    - o Know what brands and categories they are buying.
    - o Know why they are buying, functional and emotional core reasons.
    - o Know what the silent competition is for your client's discretionary spending.

- Keep The 20 Percent Happy
    - Don't get complacent.
    - Keep them happy even when they are not spending, when their tide turns they will remember you.
- Cultivate and Harvest Uncovered Opportunities
    - Discover and fill the holes in life events.
    - Build on opportunities with completing collections or missing product purchases.
    - Challenge them out of their price comfort zone and raise the bar.
    - Harness the power of emotions
    - Ask yourself, "How can I better fulfill my clients core needs?"
- Groom Tomorrow's 20 Percent
    - Some of the 80 percent are your most eager supporters.
    - They will be more appreciative of your professional, personalized service.
    - Make the most of the shorter time with undivided attention.
    - When they have more to spend, it will be with you.
- Ask For Referrals
    - A referral is very valuable and a huge compliment.
    - It is perfectly appropriate and flattering to ask your valued client for referrals.
    - Have a referral reward program.
    - Give out extra business cards to your clients.
    - Host an after hour's party for highly social, affluent clients.
- Do Not Cater To The Exceptions
    - Identify high maintenance, low return customers.
    - Don't waste your resources, save them to cultivate the rest.
- Maintain a **Killer Instinct**
    - Close the deals outside the box if needed.

Manager's Notes

Your role is to provide the needed sales history reports then assist your associates in comparing the reports with their client pages. Give them guidance on filling in the missing information and developing a follow-up plan with the client. If an associate does not wish to follow-up with a top 20 percent client of theirs, assign one that does. Also, assign the orphan clients to a well suited associate.

Develop a plan to smartly cultivate your top 20 percent. You can not expect a client to make every purchase for every life event in your store. Pick the life events that best fit your product and have the best chance of success. Contact them for these events, choosing your battles wisely. The objective is to raise their purchase frequency by one or two a year.

Use weekly one-on-one meeting with your sales staff to monitor the client book pages, the follow-up records and results. Share the success stories during your meetings to give inspiration to all.

"Coming together is a beginning. Keeping together is progress. Working together is success."

— *Henry Ford*

SUCCESS WITH TEAMWORK

There our very few tasks or jobs in any industry that could not improve in both efficiency and quality with the benefit of good teamwork. Without a doubt, the task of selling benefits greatly when we work as a team. One person cannot sell everyone, nor can everyone sell one person. We must have an atmosphere within our stores to encourage teamwork. And we must provide some procedures in place to help define our teamwork process.

Commi$$ion$ VS the Luxury Experience

Many consumers vision commissioned salespeople as money hungry swindlers. And yet I know the best service almost always comes from an associate that has a stake in the outcome of the sale and my satisfaction. A commission salesperson and a commission environment should create the best experience for the guest. Commission salespeople are the most driven, motivated, and knowledgeable on the sales floor.

So why do we have the bad rap? Have you ever heard "sounds like a used car salesperson?" What's with the stereotyping? It is simply because we at times fail to keep our clients best interests in mind as we interact with them. We might have been spouting a canned sales pitch with no personalized benefits for the guest. We might be using direct closing phrases before building enough (or any) value in our products. Or maybe we just did not listen to our guests needs. Bottom line, the guest has felt that your goal is to sell them anything you can in-order to pad your wallet.

The fact that you are being paid on commission, or get a bonus based on your sales should always be invisible to your client. We need to slow down, review the past chapters, keep our guest's needs foremost and make the client's experience luxurious. It is their needs catered to and satisfied that will in turn fulfill yours.

All Hands on Deck

Selling should not be a one-man-band. Reviewing the luxury experience you want to provide from the moment they enter the door to when they leave, there's a lot to do. And if you are providing some sort of free service, drinks, and gift wrap then there is too much for one person. Use your teammates and encourage them to use you. Make yourself available, in eye contact with your selling teammates. And do these service type tasks for free; don't ask for a split on the sale. They will in return do the same for you. End result, happier guests and happier work environment.

Team Selling

No "how to sell" book would be complete without some mention of team selling. I would assume most of us know the term **Turn-Over** or **T.O.** for short. The **T.O.** is the simple act of bringing in another sales associate to further help the guest make a buying decision. The second associate is there to sell, not just assist in a task like pouring a drink.

Unless you want to suffocate the luxury experience the guest was having, we have to be smooth and polished with our **Turn Over's**. What to **T.O.** cannot be is a high pressured way of closing the sale. Don't do it just to bring in the "hammer", or the "closer".

Many retailers have a hard and fast rule that no customer can leave (walk) without another salesperson getting a chance to sell them. While this can be a good option I will leave it up to you whether that would work in your store's environment.

So why do we want to **T.O.**? "What's in it for me?" "Why would I want to give away half of my sale?" "If I can't sell them then how would someone else?" "It's a "used car" sales trick I would not want to use." "I'm the best qualified so I don't need to **T.O.**" "The customer was just looking, they weren't ready to buy."

I hope to answer the questions and overcome these common objections to the **T.O.** Let's walk through the process step by step and explain how and why we **T.O.**

The Turn Over Process

1, Recognize the need. There are signs, clues that can be seen when you are or are not going to close a sale. Such as; you showed them two or three products and they have not shown strong interest, you can not answer their question(s), you have trial closed a couple of times receiving a negative response, they are showing negative body language, you are not making a personal connection, or you are losing your patience. There are many clues that you could add to this short list. They are stumbling blocks, minor set backs in the progression of the selling system steps. Recognize the disruption of your transition from step to step and you have indentified your need to **T.O.**

It is this need, to be able to further help the guest, that's why we **T.O.** Sometimes it is a need for more experience, but not always. It very well could be personality traits; you are not making a good connection. Other times it is your selling style; you are too forward and they need someone more laid back. Or you have just run out of ideas or ammo to sell them and need a fresh mind and face.

Whatever the reason for **Turning Over**, it needs to be done before momentum in the presentation is lost. If you have tried everything you can think of for 30 minutes, it is too late. You have exhausted yourself, the client and left nothing for the second associate. We call that **T.Oing** a body bag. Do that a few times and your teammates will scatter when they see you in need.

2, Select the correct associate. Now that you have identified the need for help; match that unfulfilled need with the sales associate that can best fill the gap. For instance; if you have run out of patience, pick the associate you know is more patient. Or if it is a matter of product knowledge, pick the associate that you know has been doing his homework. Also, don't forget the **Core Emotional Needs**. Do you need to bring someone in that can help you romance the reason to buy, or build **Emotional Value** with a good **End-Use Story**? Many times one associate can cover the technical side while another covers the emotional or romance side. Between the two associates the presentation becomes complete.

3, Nod in your T.O. partner. Many times I find the reason a salesperson didn't **T.O.** when needed was they did not know how to pause the presentation and call-in another associate. And this can be difficult even for the best of us. What I find is that when we as a team are keeping a close eye out for each other this call in becomes much easier. If we have to break our presentation and leave our guest to find another associate we blew it.

What should happen; other associates need to be a comfortable distance away but within both eye and ear contact with the selling associate when ever possible. We don't want to crowd the guest or appear like a flock of buzzards. Find a task near by and be busy but alert. If you can overhear their conversation this is even better. Then when the selling associate needs you, all that is needed is a quick nod of their head to bring you over. (Or a manager should see the nod and send another associate over or come over themselves.) As the second associate walks up we are ready for step 4.

4, Introduce. At this time you will need to break the conversation with the guest. Normally just moving eye contact from them to the second associate is all that is needed. Your conversation should go something like this; *"Bruce, come take a look at this, Mr. Guest this is Bruce."* The second associate should make eye contact with the client and shake their hand, *"Nice to meet you Mr. Guest."*

The introduction is the clear message between associates that this is a turn-over. If the selling associate said; "Bruce I have a quick question" or "Bruce can you help me?" and there is no introduction then I would take that as a request for an assist. I would then help and afterward clear away. But still be available for the chance of a **T.O.** soon.

5, Benefit the client. After the introductions we must tell the client why you have called over another associate. You should have a good reason in mind from step one and two. Let's say you have shown them three products and they don't like them so you brought over the associate that works more with some other product. Then the benefit phrase could be; "I asked Bruce over to help me assist you. He has been working in the gizmo line for years and should be of some aid."

Or if you have a scenario where the product is picked out but you can not close the sale then it might be; "I have asked Bruce over because he has personal experience with this same product." This will pour into step 6.

6, Bring needs up to speed. Flowing from the introduction, and then the benefit phrase, next is the paraphrase of the guests needs. A lot of information needs to pass in a sentence or two here. We need to give the second associate enough information to inform them of the direction and status of the sales process. Plus reinforce the benefits to the client of why we brought in the second associate. It is a key step to a smooth **T.O.**

Using the last scenario we might say; *"Bruce, Mr. Guest is thinking about presenting this gizmo to his wife for their 15th anniversary. I know you gave the same one to your wife. What was her reaction?"* In two breaths you let Bruce know the **Functional Need** for purchase, that the product has been chosen, the direction you want Bruce to take, and what **Core Emotion** Bruce needs to work.

As associates work together they can develop a form of silent communication to help with the **T.O.** transition. For instance; if I have a guest deciding between more than one product, I will touch or hold one the products in my right hand. The one in the right is the one I want the other associate to lead the client into buying. It might have been the one I was recommending and I don't want **my T.O.** partner contradicting my sales pitch. Or it might be the product I know the client likes but just needs another opinion. You might want to add your own silent communications to further your team's effectiveness.

We have kept this communication short and condensed. We don't want to give too much information to the other associate. I have seen at times the first associate informing the second all the products they have shown, which one the client likes and dislikes, what the client's objections are, the guest's price range, or a complete list of features and benefits they have told the client. You do not want to speak of any of these things for two reasons. One, the client does not want to stand there and listen to you fill-in this new associate, you are wasting their time and airing their dirty laundry in a sense. Two, the largest benefit of the **T.O.** would be lost. Let me explain.

People shop and compare. They gather information and opinions. When we **T.O.** with just enough information to give the second associate some direction, we leave the opportunity open for a **Candid Second Opinion**. So the second associate might show the same products, and most likely present many of the same features and benefits you have. And this is great! It is just what you want them to do. It will reinforce what you have recommended and said. So many times this is what makes the difference and closes the sale.

Statistically consumers buy from the third salesperson they talk to. So if they have been one other place and talked to one sales associate your **T.O.** partner just became the third and lucky salesperson. Think about it; when your **Two Candid Opinions** come together they win against your competition's one opinion. And the client's fact gathering need is fulfilled. They feel comfortable to make an informed buying decision. Also if the client has not been elsewhere they might still feel the need to get another opinion. When we T.O. we provide that **Candid Second Opinion** and increase our chances of closing the sale by two, or more. If we let them walk with out a **T.O.** we **T.O.** them and our sale to our competition.

Another reason we do not want to overly inform the second associate is that we might discourage your **T.O.** partner. If you have informed them of all the products shown, benefits stated, and the client's objections, it would discourage them to repeat your presentation. We want them to go in fresh and positive. We should not inform them of the client's price range either. Let the associate discover the price range.

I have experienced several times when the second associate sells well above the price range that was given from the client to the first associate. This happens because the T.O. partner goes in with no inhibitions.

7, Graceful exit. A turn over is when we smoothly introduce another associate and allow them to take over the selling process. It becomes a very different scenario if the first selling associate does not leave. Remember, we want the second associate to reshow and retell what we have done. And we want the client to be able to get that **Candid Second Opinion**. If the first associate stays with the guest this becomes difficult. How it is perceived by the client is that he now has two salespeople ganging up on him. There can be exceptions to this and I will cover them below. But most of the time the first associate should gracefully bow out.

In-order to make a graceful exit we need to excuse ourselves. The best reason and one we should always try to use is a service to the client validation. Say; "Mr. Guest, while Bruce tells you his wife's story, I'll clean your ring" or "Mr. Guest, while Bruce demonstrates this widget I'll check current inventory on these products." Don't ask for permission, make it a service and just do it.

So putting steps 4, 5, 6 and 7 smoothly together would have something that sounds like this. Associate #1, Mandy says; "Bruce, come take a look at this, Mr. Guest this is Bruce." Bruce should make eye contact with the client and shake their hand saying, "Nice to meet you Mr. Guest." Mandy states; "I have asked Bruce over because he has personal experience with this same product. Bruce, Mr. Guest is thinking about presenting this diamond ring to his wife for their 15th anniversary. I know you gave the same one to your wife, and her reaction is a great story. Mr. Guest, while Bruce tells you his wife's story, I'll clean your ring." Guest says; "thank you Mandy. Bruce you gave this to your wife? She is one lucky lady." Bruce says; "Mr. Guest, your wife will be too, let me tell you how I presented it to her…"

8, Ready for an assist. Now that you have made your exit don't come back until asked. Clean the ring or check on stock until the other associate asks you for the results. This gives them a chance to do their job. This is not a time to take a break or go to lunch. You are now partnered up on this sale and you owe it to your teammate to assist them as needed. Or you need to sell for them, more on that later. Stay on the sales floor, stay looking busy, and stay in eye contact with your **T.O.** partner.

When the sale is closed, assist with writing up the ticket and praise the client on his good choice. And you or your teammate should ask for the add-on sale. Again, just be careful that you don't gang up two against one. Also, this is a good time to fill out a client page and add to a wish list. All of this becomes much easier as a team.

Turn Over VS Team Sell

A **Team Sell** is when you and the second sales associate stay with the guest during the sales presentation. I recommend that you use the **T.O.** (with the first associate making a clean exit) for most of your selling scenarios. Again it will provide a more candid presentation and an uninhibited selling process. But there can be some exceptions to this rule.

A couple shopping together can be at times more than one associate can handle by themselves. In many instances one associate can be showing style or design to the lady while the other associate talks features, quality, and price with the man. Then as a team you can bring them together and close the sale. Or I have quietly taken the buying half of the party to the cash wrap to make the purchase. Then they can surprise the other with a spontaneous "it's yours!"

Another time an associate was helping the lady in the diamond department while I had the man in the watch department. I took the man over to have him show his lady the timepiece he selected. She in turn showed him her ring of choice. They bought both on impulse because of each others excitement.

Many people shop with a friend. Sometimes a friend can help with the sale process, but many times they are the critic. Another associate can draw away the critic, taking them to another department or showcase. Then the goal is to loosen up the critic, win them over with a service or perk and make them your allied. Or you might just sell the friend something of their own. Then they would encourage the other to do the same.

Everywhere There Are Signs

A good sign that you need a **Team Sell** or **T.S.** is when the shopping friend or spouse wanders away from the other and you. I believe no guest should wander or shop without being asked if they would like some help. At the very least, offer them a drink and have a casual conversation. Then see if you can direct them back into the selling process. This process is how we made the watch and diamond ring sale earlier.

So how do you communicate in front of the customers when you want to **Turn Over** vs. **Team Sell**? If you want to **Turn Over,** make your exit service statement. If you want the other associate to stay, keep your body facing openly between the guest(s) and the associate. If you want them to leave, face the client(s), putting your side to the associate. Also eye contact can be used to direct an associate to a straying shopping partner. All floor staff needs to stay alert for these signals.

Above all, have fun with **Team Selling**. Keep the energy high and the guest relaxed with the attention you give them. Your job will be more enjoyable and more rewarding.

Key Points

- The task of selling will benefit in both efficiency and quality by utilizing your team members effectively.
- We must have a store atmosphere that encourages teamwork.
- Our clients' best interests must be first and foremost in our minds as we sell.
- The fact that we are paid on commission must be invisible to our clients.
- We should all be available and alert on the sales floor for an assist or **T.O.**
- Use your teammates and persuade them to use you for free assists.
- Don't use the **T.O.** to bring in the hard closer. Bring them in to benefit the client.
- Statistically consumers buy from the third salesperson. Increase your odds 100% with a smooth **T.O.** and giving your client **Candid Second Opinions**.
- Use the **Team Sell** with multiple shopping friends or wandering spouses.
- If we don't **T.O.** to our teammates we **T.O.** to our competition.
- Have fun with the **Turn Over** and **Team Selling**. Make it fun and relaxed for your clients. Enjoy your job!

Manager's Notes

In-order for all of our guests to have a consistent **Luxury Experience** and to encourage teamwork on the sales floor I propose some sales floor guidelines. Using the **T.O.** and **T.S.** processes plus many of the luxury experience lessons in previous chapters I will outline how I have run my sales floors for best team effectiveness. Please look at the Sales Floor Etiquette below.

You and your assistants will need to be on the sales floor, as the floor managers. You should help insure that everyone is assisted, the right salesperson is with the right client, and they have a teammate standing by to assist or take a **T.O.** if needed.

And it probably goes without me saying it again, but this lesson will take a lot of practice, almost certainly the most of any in this book. We need to make it so smooth that the guest sees it only as a benefit and service. A service they will want time and time again.

Steps to the T.O.

1. **Recognize the need.**
    i. Do it before momentum in the presentation is lost.
2. **Select the correct associate.**
    i. Use the best associate that can fill the gap in client needs.
3. **Nod in your T.O. partner.**
    i. The key to this step is floor awareness on the part of the non-selling associates and maintaining eye contact with the selling associates.
4. **Introduce.**
    i. Introducing is the clear message that this is a **T.O.**
    ii. If you don't introduce than you must only want a quick assist.
5. **Benefit the client.**
    i. Use a **Benefit Statement** of why you called over the second associate.
6. **Bring needs up to speed.**
    i. In a couple sentences you need to paraphrase the client's needs and give the second associate just enough info for direction.

ii. This is the key to a smooth **T.O.** that closes sales.
   iii. Develop a few ways to communicate silently with your **T.O.** partners; like the right hand method.
   iv. Leave opportunity for the **Candid Second Opinion**.
   v. Don't tell your **T.O.** partner anything that would inhibit them or the selling process.
7. **Graceful exit.**
   i. Provide a service to the client with your departure.
8. **Ready for an assist.**
   i. Make yourself available for your **T.O.** partner or sell for them. Have eye contact.
   ii. Don't come back until your **T.O.** partner nods you back. Then help with the paperwork.

Sales Floor Etiquette

- One management person stays free to oversee and run the sales floor at all times. He or she directs traffic, making sure the right salesperson is with the right client. They must stay aware of how each presentation is going and who is needed for an assist or **T.O.**, and keeping the non-selling associates ready for teamwork. Interaction with guests should be on their side of the counter or displays, leaving the salesperson to make the presentation.
- Associates are spread out on the sales floor. No gathering for conversations and no lurking at the door waiting for the next victim. Stay busy with cleaning, merchandise display, client books, and phone calls. Also, have some associates on the guests' side of the counters to give the look of more store traffic if slow. This is a good time to team up for sales role-plays. A single associate should greet their guest coming in to avoid the vulture experience.
- Welcome each guest using your store name. Ask them if they have been in before. And if so, ask them if they have a preferred sales associate. This will go a long way to prevent internal conflict with your fellow staff and to give the guest the best service.

- **T.O.** any sale that you can not close today with money down.
- Make yourself available for assists and **T.O.** Keep in eye and ear contact as much as possible, but don't crowd.
- Maintain floor awareness, knowing whose guest is whose and what is happing with them.
- Drink pouring and other services are freebies; don't expect a split on the sale.
- Don't gang up on a guest; never have more than two associates with a guest at a time. If there is a third or more they should be stepping out to provide a service for the guest.
- Stay available to your selling **T.O.** partner if they need help or service. Do not go on a break.
- When you help other guests while you have **T.O.ed** to another associate the following rule applies; you are "tied" or "married" to you **T.O.** partner. Any sales resulting from the time of the **T.O.** to the time you are both free are split with each other. If a third associate is involved with one of the sales than that sale alone is split three ways.
- The client page and follow-up goes to the original, first sales associate; unless it is agreed that because of a better rapport it goes to the other. You can work a client together but one needs to be the lead and insure that the follow up is completed.
- Be-back clients should be directed to the original associate for further help. If unavailable, help their guest and only take a split if you made a professional sales presentation that made the difference in the guest purchasing. If they leave again without buying report the visit and any new info to their salesperson.
- No one can own a guest, only a guest can claim a salesperson. Remember to ask guests if they have a preferred associate and you will be covered.
- When in doubt of any situation, talk to your teammate first, before coming to a manager. This will help build trust, respect and team spirit with your mates.

Wow, that's a lot of rules. These are the most I have ever used. Many times I have not needed them all and then at times it seems like I need more. But you cannot write rules to cover every scenario or make rules just because of one bad egg. Use what you want from the list, if any. As long as there is a system in place to provide consistency then fairness should travel in a full circle.

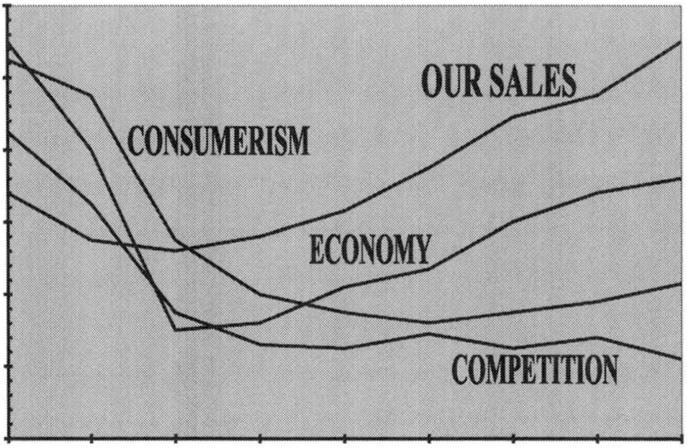
OUR SALES
CONSUMERISM
ECONOMY
COMPETITION

SELLING AGAINST THE INTERNET

The internet has now been around for awhile. Some of us working adults grew up with the internet and then some of us have yet to use it in our everyday lives. What none of us can do though is ignore its existence. Seventy percent of the people in North America use the internet in some manner. We need to embrace its technology and utilize its resources.

The internet has also caused a stir in the way many consumers shop and buy. But I do not believe it replaces many of the traditional "brick and mortar" stores. You can buy anything off the internet, but do you want to? That's a key question we all should ask.

What's New about the Internet?

We have had "internet" type competition since the 1890's, ever since Sears and Roebuck (amongst others) prospered in business shipping goods to all 38 states and our territories. They beat out the local general stores by dealing in volume and using the railroad and postal service to deliver the lower cost goods. And they weren't the last company prospering in the mail order business. In the early 80's I managed and sold at a specialty camera store. We had no internet. We hardly had personal computers. But we did have large mail-order firms advertising in all the photography magazines with prices at or below my cost. You can still see their ads in these magazines and they are online. Today we also have warehouse stores driving down prices in name brand products. All of these sources rely on only one thing to sell products and that is lower prices.

But with any of these sources are the products really the same? Can we trust the company? How long will I wait for my product? What do we have to do if we have problems after the sale? What's the final cost of my purchase? These are questions on the mind of most when dealing with price cutting sources. And there are other questions they should be asking. Let's take a look at them all.

Questions on Their Mind

Am I getting the same product? Many times you are getting the same product. But if you were to search the internet for the lowest possible price and bought it, I would guess you will not get an identical product. Possible deviations could be, older last years model, reconditioned, used, returned and resold, blemished, defective, fake copy, unauthorized manufacture, shop worn, opened packaging, no warranty, or inferior quality. When it comes to the lowest price; "if it seems too good to be true, it probably is."

Many better quality manufactures do not allow their products to be sold online. They also might have a policy against shipping their products over state lines. This helps protect the lines integrity and the dealer's territory. A signed agreement between the manufactures and its dealers creates these policies. Then when you do see it online you know it must not be from an authorized source, a source that can not be trusted. You might already carry merchandise from companies that practice these procedures. Ask next time you are looking for a new line.

The specs read the same, so is it the same? I am an analytical like many cautious shoppers, so I love specifications. But I have found that in all products there is a lack of consistency in how specs are derived and passed on. You can not trust them and they cannot tell the whole story of any product. Steer away from selling any of your products using specs. Use personable experiences, **End-Use** and **Life Moments** to sell, not made up numbers on paper. Besides, do we carry the big window sticker from our new car, whipping it out when someone asks? No, we take the friend for a ride so they can experience the car for what it is, not for what the sticker said. It's all about **End-Use Moments**.

Can I trust the company? Any company is only as good as the people working for it. And the only person you can trust to follow thru with all promises made is yourself. Build that same trust with your guest and they won't want to go elsewhere.

They have a great website with lots of inventory so they must be a big, honest company, right? Not necessarily. Many companies are just the website you see, nothing more. They don't have a store or warehouse. The inventory you see on their website is not owned by them. In truth they may not own any merchandise. They are a middleman selling from a manufacture's or distributer's inventory. Then the product is drop shipped directly from the manufacture. Receipts and labels might even read from the website company, but that is done by agreement with the distributor. This can cause many problems with prompt delivery and return of products.

Who is going to help me make the right choice? One of the most obvious drawbacks to buying online is not getting to see, hold, or test the products before you purchase. And having an educated and helpful salesperson can save a lot of time and frustrations. So the best help a consumer can find in making that choice will be from you.

Am I informed enough to buy on-line? The internet does offer a huge opportunity and source for research. In the comfort of your office or home you can research all products. You can read manufacture's claims, see 360 degree photos, and decipher actual consumer reviews. Then you can find dealers, compare prices, and check inventory stock. The internet is a powerful tool and many of your best customers use it. But as long as you offer a better overall value for their money then they will not use the internet to buy.

There have been many times I have had guests shopping with me when I suspect they are comparing products against the internet. You can often tell by the questions they ask and the lack of buying signals. Some will want the help in making the right product choice and come to you for that service. They get to see, hold, and try your products. Then leave without buying, but buy online at a lesser price. At anytime you feel a guest is comparing you to any competition ask them. Just be direct, but with a helpful tone. Say; "let me help you make some comparisons, where else have you been looking?" Once they tell you they have been shopping on the internet you can both precede thru the shopping process with no hidden agendas. Then it is your job to build value in your product, company, and your services above the price.

Sell, don't teach. Be careful that you don't just educate them so they can buy online. Hold back some product use information, but tell them that you will share some key product features and instructions once they buy.

How long do I have to wait for my product? Good question. Yes you will wait. Then you'll wonder if it will be safe on your doorstep or if someone will be able to sign for a package. Or you might have to take a long lunch break to go to the post office. If it was out of stock you might want to ask for your money back, wait the ten days to receive the refund and then start over.

But if you buy from us you can take the product home today and enjoy. Why wait?

What if I have problems after the purchase? Well I hope you got a factory fresh and current model. If it's not exactly what you expected are you going through the hassle and expense to send it back? At the very least it will mean a trip to the post office and a few bucks from your wallet. Then follow up with a few phone calls and that good deal is more than gone. So you end up living with a inferior product and/or added expenses and frustrations.

As a customer friendly brick and mortar store we can offer a full return or exchange service. And can handle any product service you may need.

What other perks do I get with my online purchase? Packing peanuts, but if you bought from us you would have this whole book full of perks.

Will my wife/husband be impressed? When buying a gift the internet is not your best choice. The process of shopping, choosing, purchasing, and wrapping a gift for a loved one is a romantic act. It is not all about what you give, but what you did to acquire the gift. Most gift receivers would rather be given a gift purchased from a local, respected retail store. Buying from the internet makes one look cheap and lazy.

What is the final price of my purchase? In addition to the advertised price they have packing, shipping, and insurance. Then add your time away from the office to pick up the package at the post office. Then when something is not just right, another trip to the post office, double the time and expenses.

If you would like to buy from your local retailer you can spare these expenses and headaches.

Where does my money go? Your money will immediately go into an out of town bank account, gaining interest while they get around to finding and shipping your product. Then what they do with the money is none of your business.

"If you buy from us then your money will stay in the local economy. We employee local residents that our involved within our community. Our company also sponsors a local little league team and donates to a girl scout troop yearly." What ever your story is, I am sure it can be much better than the mail-order company across the country.

Plant the Seed of Doubt

There are more questions and more answers. I will leave it up to you to address the ones that fit your particularly business. But what all these questions add up to is doubt. Doubt that the consumer is getting what they want and need and if they are getting the best price and value.

What we need to do is plant that seed of doubt in a non-internet-bashing way. Use any combination of these questions and start the conversation with your guest, like; "Dave, have you given any thought to where your money goes when you buy off the internet? If you buy from us it stays in our local economy to get recirculated into our community. That is important, right?" Or state; "Dave, I cannot match the price of the one you saw on the internet, but I can, as an authorized dealer guarantee that my products come with the full manufactures warranty and are factory fresh, current models. Plus we have for 30 years stood behind our products with our service. OK?"

The client may not have thought of the entire drawback to the internet purchase, or weighed the benefits of buying local. It is our job to help them make an informed buying decision. We need to bring these questions up and plant that seed of doubt.

Knowledge is Power

Savvy consumers can educate themselves with a few clicks of a mouse. And that is the real power of the net. Many times I see consumers more informed than the salesperson trying to sell a product. If we can not impress them with our knowledge and wow them with service then they will shop elsewhere.

Do your research. Know your products and know your competition. Spend some time shopping your internet competition. Know their prices, added costs, return and exchange policies, and delivery schedules. Know what ones are authorized dealers and question the ones that aren't. Use the Web to do research, for both yours and your competitions' product. The more you know the better you can sell against the internet.

If You Can't Beat Them, Join Them

At this point any business that wants to flourish should have a website of your own. Many successful brick and mortar stores have bridged the gap between their way of business and the internet. They have done this with an information only Web site. I enjoy reading company history and learning company philosophy on these sites. I find out about the products they sell and the services they offer. I might even be able to read client testimonials.

Without you having an internet presence many consumers won't know who or where you are. I never keep a phone book in my home or office. I go online. When I look for a branded product I look on the web for local dealers. And I choose a local dealer based on the findings online. You should also check into search engine placements. If I search for your product by brand name or type, I would want to find you listed high on the first page. This is marketing money well spent.

You don't have to sell on the internet. Inform your potential clients that your company chooses to maintain a personalized way of doing business. You staff your store with the best people and train then to provide the best customer service and that you prefer doing business one-on-one, face-to-face. Share information of how your business supports the local economy and community. Post photos of your store hosting a chartable event. Or have a blog on community involvement of your staff. You can add more pages as you go. You just need to get online and join the fun.

Key Points

- You can't ignore the internet, 70% of consumers use it.
- We must utilize its resources and develop techniques to sell against it.
- Internet, mail-order, and warehouse stores all sell on price alone. We have so much more to offer.
- Consumers can educate themselves with a few mouse clicks, we need to stay ahead of them and do the same, and more. Know your products and competition.
- Plant the seed of doubt. Bring the questions up for discussion and sell your benefits and peace of mind.
- Sell the product's benefits and end use moments, not the paper specs.
- Sell, do not teach. Hold back teaching about a product until the client buys. Make how-to instructions a perk for buying from you.
- To compete against the internet you need to be on the internet. Have a web site that will inform the consumer why they should shop with you. Make sure they find you when they search.
- Every lesson in this book is how to sell against the internet, and any other discount source.

Manager's Notes

Like any new sales technique this one will take some practice to smooth the rough edges. Make sure that we approach the seed of doubt planting in a professional manner. Anytime we directly bash our competition we will loose respect with our guests. But if we build up our positive benefits and suggest the internet or other competition might lack these benefits we can be subtle and more effective.

Make up a list with you team of all the reasons your clients should shop and buy with you. Use the list of doubt questions, adding to the list any others that you have in your business. Answer these questions with positive benefits your company offers. Then use these in role-plays until smooth.

Encourage yourself and your staff to shop the online competition. It will reinforce that they are selling for the better side and they will become stronger salespeople.

CREATE YOUR CULTURE AND LIVE YOUR DREAM

Your store culture is created by what you do everyday. In-order for it to prosper it needs a direction or clear path and a goal or destination. The destination and its path are defined within three documents. They are your **Vision Statement**, **Mission Statement**, and **Service Standards**. End result, this all becomes your **Company Culture**. We need to take a look at what you have now and review, rewrite or write these three documents. It's a tall order, but if you have read this book and hopefully learned and implemented many of the lessons you are well on your way. This chapter will wrap up the things that have made you successful in the past with the new guest services and sales procedures you have learned from this book. Let's take this a step at a time.

Vision Statement

Back when you first started thinking of opening, buying, or managing your own business you had a dream. This dream or vision painted a picture of what you thought your business would become. If you were to take your dream and sum up the most important elements into one sentence, this would be your business's **Vision Statement**.

I will give you my company's **Vision Statement** as an example; *I envision offering innovative training products and programs that will excite, motivate, and advance good salespeople to higher excellence.* I hope I have lived up to this vision so far. A retail stores **Vision Statement** could be; *We envision to become the most consumer respected and highest volume source for our products in the Northwest.* The statement clearly tells of the company's goal and gives us something to work towards achieving.

If you have a **Vision Statement** already, great! Just review it and make sure it still aligns with your current dream and is relevant to your daily work. If you don't then close your eyes, dream a little and write it down in one clear sentence. Then once done, print it and share it with all staff members.

You might be reading this book because your business has not yet fulfilled your vision. Read on and we will take even the loftiest dream and break it down to easy daily steps to achieve your dream.

Mission Statement

A **Mission Statement** is a short list of what your company will strive to do and offer to achieve the **Company Vision Statement**. It is the big picture of your unique business philosophy. It is the list of great things you believe in as a business person and you will proudly post on your retail floor. It defines your **Culture**.

A retail store's **Mission Statement** might read;

Acme Retailer will always be on the leading edge with top quality, innovative, and fashionable products.

We will uncompromisingly offer the best products while maintaining fair prices.

We will uphold the highest standards of product knowledge in our industry to give our clients the most informed and candid advice.

We will provide consistently high customer service before, during and after the sale.

We will stay dynamically involved in our community and return profits to our local economy.

So just like your **Vision Statement**, write and/or review your **Mission Statement**. Does it outline your **Vision Statement**? Is there more you can add or something that no longer fits? Can you proudly display it in your store? And are you and everyone in your company living up to it?

The next step will be the means of living up to your mission statement and achieving your vision.

Service Standards

We have our **Mission Statement** outlining our **Company Vision**. Now we need to know what to do during our workday to achieve our vision and align with our mission. Again, **Service Standards** is a list of actions all company associates, managers, and owners need to follow in-order for our guests to experience our company's vision and mission statements. It will become our everyday life and create our **Culture**.

Your **Service Standards** should sum up the actions needed by all employees so your guests receive your **Luxury Experience**. It may make mention of key steps to a sale, but only as perceived by the guest. IE; *"We will utilize all our resources and teammates to assist our guests to the best of our abilities."* Not; *"We will T.O. all customers that we can not close."* Though the former might lead to the later, we want it to read and always perceived as benefiting our guest.

To help form your list, take a good look at your steps to a sale. And take a look at the chapter lessons in this book. From the moment the guest parks their car to the moments the client enjoys their product, we have the opportunity to enhance their experience with our **Service Standards**. Think about that complete experience and summarize how we are going to help provide the **Luxury Experience**.

My example of **Service Standards** would read:

We will maintain positive attitudes and reflect a positive business position at all times.

We will create an **Oasis** *with in our store that guests will want to come and escape from life's frustrations.*

We will consistently offer all guests a drink and our added free service each time they visit.

We will flatter and excite all guests by showing them our most impressive styles. We will **Dazzle** *them.*

We will never prejudge. Every guest will get the same **Luxury Experience**.

We will give our guests our complete attention, listen well, and cater to their **Core Needs**.

We will maintain effective **Luxury Experience Client Books** *with wish lists and life events to benefit our clients.*

We will under-promise and over-deliver with all orders. And we will maintain flawless follow-up with our clients.

We will utilize all forms of communications as preferred by our clients in a prompt and professional manner.

We will maintain the highest level of product knowledge, above and beyond our competition.

We will stay well informed of our marketplace and our competition in-order to serve our clients.

We will utilize all our resources and our teammates to assist our guests to the best of our abilities.

Live Your Dream

Once we have all three, your **Vision Statement**, **Mission Statement**, and **Service Standards** agreed and written, you are prepared. You are ready to establish you **New Business Culture**. I would have all three professionally printed and framed. You should post all three in the back office for management and employees to see. The **Mission Statement** and **Service Standards** post in the break room for associates to see daily. Then a proud copy of the **Mission Statement** should be displayed on the sales floor for your guests. You should also post the **Mission Statement** on your Web site.

Use these documents everyday, from new employee orientation, to monthly and yearly staff reviews, and daily inspirations. Many companies also ask their employees to memorize at least the **Mission Statement**. And you should follow thru with your **Service Standards** at all times. You could even have everyone sign the copies to be framed and hung.

You are now aligned. You have a clear understanding, and well communicated throughout your company of what your attentions are. You have a plan, a process to achieve your attentions. You have created your **Culture**. Now enjoy your dream.

Key Points

- A **Vision Statement** tells your business dream.
- A **Mission Statement** defines your culture to achieve your dream. Post it proudly in your store.
- **Service Standards** become your everyday life and creates your **culture**. Follow thru and live it.
- These three documents are the clear path and destination of your business.
- Your Vision and Mission may change overtime. Keep them updated if needed.
- **Service Standards** should never stale. Keep up with the changing business and consumer environments.
- **Service Standards** should read and always perceived as benefiting your guest.
- **Service Standards** lead to a **Luxury Experience**.
- Use these documents with new employee training, staff reviews, and daily inspirations.
- You are aligned with your plan. You created your **Culture**. Now enjoy your dream.

Manager's Notes

After these three documents are written, signed, hung, and even memorized your job will be to teach and remind. You have to teach and remind every day. You cannot just say it once and expect it to be done. This goes for **Service Standards** and any other lesson or sales procedure. Even after months of doing the same thing if you let you guard down we will get lazy. Remind and re-teach as needed every day. Be fair and consistent, follow up and praise, offer help and encouragement, and praise again.

For every book that you read or training you attend, you should learn and utilize at least one lesson. I hope you have been able to do just that or more with my book. Never stop learning.

Kind regards,

Bruce